A Short Introduction to
Attachment
and
Attachment
Disorder

of related interest

Nurturing Attachments
Supporting Children who are Fostered or Adopted
Kim S. Golding
ISBN 978 1 84310 614 2

Big Steps for Little People
Parenting Your Adopted Child
Celia Foster
Forewords by David Howe and Daniel A. Hughes
ISBN 978 1 84310 620 3

Life Story Books for Adopted Children
A Family Friendly Approach
Joy Rees
Foreword by Alan Burnell
Illustrated by Jamie Goldberg
ISBN 978 1 84310 953 2

Understanding Attachment and Attachment Disorders
Theory, Evidence and Practice
Vivien Prior and Danya Glaser
ISBN 978 1 84310 245 8

Children and Spirituality
Searching for Meaning and Connectedness
Brendan Hyde
ISBN 978 1 84310 589 3

The Colors of Grief
Understanding a Child's Journey through Loss from Birth to Adulthood
Janis A. Di Ciacco
ISBN 978 1 84310 886 3

Cool Connections with Cognitive Behavioural Therapy
Encouraging Self-esteem, Resilience and Well-being in Children and Young People Using CBT Approaches
Laurie Seiler
ISBN 978 1 84310 618 0

Feeling Like Crap
Young People and the Meaning of Self-Esteem
Nick Luxmoore
ISBN 978 1 84310 682 1

Colby Pearce

A Short Introduction to
Attachment
and
Attachment
Disorder

Jessica Kingsley Publishers
London and Philadelphia

First published in 2009
by Jessica Kingsley Publishers
116 Pentonville Road
London N1 9JB, UK
and
400 Market Street, Suite 400
Philadelphia, PA 19106, USA

www.jkp.com

Library of Congress Cataloging in Publication Data
Pearce, Colby.
A short introduction to attachment and attachment disorder / Colby Pearce.
p. cm.
Includes bibliographical references and index.
ISBN 978-1-84310-957-0 (pb : alk. paper) 1. Attachment disorder in children. 2.
Attachment behavior in children. I. Title.
RJ507.A77.P43 2009
618.92'8588--dc22

2008049609

British Library Cataloguing in Publication Data
A CIP catalogue record for this book is available from the British Library

ISBN 978 1 84310 957 0

Printed and bound in Great Britain by
MPG Books Limited, Cornwall

03 11

To all the children I have known and their caregivers.
You have been my inspiration.

ACKNOWLEDGEMENTS

The author wishes to acknowledge Dr Graham Martin and Glenys Forrester, who gave the author his first meaningful employment opportunities in child and family mental health, without which this book would never have been written.

The author also wishes to acknowledge Patricia Rayment and Kylie Eitzen for valuable collaboration along the journey.

In addition, the writer wishes to acknowledge Claire Simmons for her helpful advice regarding the manuscript, and for her words of encouragement.

The writer further wishes to acknowledge Rebecca, Thomas, Lachlan and Hamish, who are his secure base.

CONTENTS

Chapter 1
Understanding Attachment 13

What is attachment? (13); What are the origins of Attachment Theory? (14); What is the role of attachment? (16); How does attachment develop? (19); What does attachment look like? (19); What different types of attachment exist? (20); How does caregiving impact on attachment? (24); Matthew's story (26); Chapter summary (29)

Chapter 2
Understanding Attachment Disorder 31

What is attachment disorder? (31); What are attachment representations? (35); What is the contribution of arousal and over-arousal? (39); What is the significance of parental accessibility? (44); How do I know if a child has an attachment disorder? (49); What does attachment disorder look like? (51); Matthew's story (continued) (53); Chapter summary (54)

Chapter 3
Parenting the Attachment-Disordered Child 57

The importance of promoting strong and secure attachment relationships (57); First principles (59); Addressing accessibility preoccupations (61); Changes in attachment representations (70); Managing arousal (79); Putting it all together (79); Additional considerations (83); Matthew's story (continued) (83); Chapter summary (88)

Chapter 4
Treating the Attachment-Disordered Child –

What constitutes effective treatment? (89); A strengths perspective (91); Caregiver participation in psychotherapy (92); Some secrets about how attachment-disordered children can be engaged in psychotherapy (93); Matthew's story (continued) (96); Chapter summary (97)

A SHORT INTRODUCTION

Conventional wisdom tells us that if something walks like a duck and talks like a duck it must be a duck. That is, if it *behaves* like a duck it must be a duck. Once we have established that something is a duck, our knowledge and experience with ducks tells us what we can expect from the duck and how to relate to it. But what if it looks like a duck but *thinks* like a swan, because it became separated from its mother and father duck and was raised by a swan? Would our expectations regarding its behaviour still be valid? Would we, upon knowing that the duck thought like a swan, relate to it as if it were a duck?

I wrote this book because I believe that it is not *what* children do, but *why* they do it that is crucial to understanding them, relating effectively with them and, where required, intervening successfully with them. This distinction between what children do and why they do it is crucial to the accurate diagnosis of childhood mental disorders and their appropriate and effective treatment. In order to understand why children behave the way they do, one needs to know something of the ways in which they think and the historical circumstances that shaped the ways they think.

All who are involved with children in a caregiving role will be able to access in this book information about how children's early care experiences shape their character. In particular, the reader will be able to access information about the thought processes and preoccupations that give rise to perplexing and challenging behaviour and emotional displays in children who have an early history of inadequate and/or problematic care, as well as strategies to promote more helpful thoughts about self, other and the world. It is anticipated that having a better understanding of why attachment-disordered children behave in the way that they do will assist their caregivers to relate effectively, and intervene successfully, with them, so that these children may attain the fundamental precursors to a full and satisfying life: believing that the world is a safe place, that they are capable, that they are lovable and deserving of love, and that relationships with others are rewarding.

Throughout the book I make reference to one gender or other when exemplifying the concepts I am presenting. Unless I state otherwise, I do not intend for the reader to think that the concepts under discussion are gender-specific. Rather, I have generally referred to one gender or the other for ease of reading. Similarly, I would draw the reader's attention to the glossary at the end of this book. The glossary is included to inform and clarify my own interpretation of various terms included in this book, and is reflective of my general endeavour to make the subject matter of the book accessible to the broadest audience possible. As such, it is not intended to be a glossary for professional use only. Rather, I anticipate that the glossary will assist in ensuring that all readers attain a full and satisfying understanding of my experiences and perspectives concerning attachment and attachment disorder.

Colby Pearce
April 2009

PROLOGUE

Once upon a time there were three mice. The first mouse lived in a house that contained, along with furniture and other household goods and possessions, a button and a hole in the wall from which food was delivered. Each time the mouse pressed the button he would receive a tasty morsel of his favourite food. The mouse understood that, when he was hungry, all he had to do was press the button and food would arrive via the hole. The mouse took great comfort in the predictability of his access to food and only pressed the button when he was hungry.

The second mouse lived in a similar house, also containing a button and a hole in the wall from which food was delivered. Unfortunately, the button in his house was faulty and delivered food on a inconsistent basis when he pressed it, such that he might only receive food via the hole on the first, fifth, seventh, or even the eleventh time he pressed the button. This mouse learnt that he could not always rely on the button and that he had to press the button many times, even when he was not actually hungry, in order to ensure that he would have food. Even after his button was fixed he found it difficult to stop pressing it frequently and displayed a habit of storing up food.

The third mouse also lived in a similar house, containing a button and a hole in the wall from which food was to be delivered. However, the button in his house did not work at all.

He soon learnt that he could not rely on the button and would have to develop other ways of gaining access to food. This belief persisted, even when he moved to a new home with a fully functioning button.

CHAPTER 1

UNDERSTANDING ATTACHMENT

WHAT IS ATTACHMENT?

'Attachment' is a term used to describe the dependency relationship a child develops towards his or her primary caregivers. It is first observable during the latter half of the first year of life and develops progressively over the first four years of life. It is most readily observed in the behaviour of children when they are sick, injured, tired, anxious, hungry or thirsty.

Although early attachment research focused on the mother–infant dyad, it is now generally accepted that children form multiple attachment relationships. An 'attachment figure' is defined as someone who provides physical and emotional care, has continuity and consistency in the child's life, and who has an emotional investment in the child's life.[1] This can include parents (biological, foster, adopted), grandparents, siblings, aunts and uncles, and alternate caregivers (e.g. child-care workers).

Given that children are able to form multiple attachments, the question has been asked as to which attachment relationship is most influential on children's developmental outcomes.

The literature provides considerable support for the integrative model of attachment: that is, children's social–emotional development is best predicted by their network of attachment figures rather than by a single attachment relationship *per se*.[2]

WHAT ARE THE ORIGINS OF ATTACHMENT THEORY?

During the 1930s and '40s, psychoanalytically oriented clinicians in the US and Europe were making observations of the ill-effects on personality development of prolonged institutional care and frequent changes of mother-figure during the first years of life. Among them was a psychiatrist who, prior to receiving his medical training, had studied developmental psychology. His name was John Bowlby.

At this time mainstream psychoanalytic thought argued that infants develop a close bond to their mother because she feeds them. Two kinds of drive were postulated: primary and secondary. Food was thought of as primary, the personal relationship (referred to as 'dependency') as secondary. Bowlby believed that this did not fit with his observations. For if it were true, an infant of one or two years of age would take readily to whomever fed him, and this clearly was not the case. It was also inconsistent with emerging empirical evidence from animal studies, including the work of Harry Harlow.[3] In his studies, Harlow separated infant rhesus monkeys from their mothers within 6–12 hours of birth and raised them with the aid of two forms of 'mother surrogate'. In one condition, the cage in which the infant rhesus monkey was accommodated contained a warm, soft 'mother surrogate'. This mother surrogate was shaped to feel like a mother, was wrapped in towelling to make it soft, was warmed by a light bulb placed behind it, and incorporated an artificial teat from which the infant nursed. The other mother surrogate was the same in every way, except that it was made of wire. What it lacked was softness. Harlow found that the infant rhesus monkeys with the warm, soft mother surrogate sought and maintained contact with it, whereas the infants with the wire mother surrogate did not. In addition, the infants with the soft, warm mother surrogate thrived, whereas the infants with the wire mother surrogate did not. Furthermore, all infant rhesus monkeys displayed an apparent attachment to a heated gauze pad placed in the bottom of their cage and became distressed when this was removed, further emphasising the importance of contact comfort in the development of attachment bonds over physical nourishment alone.

During the 1950s, Bowlby, with the assistance of a number of research associates working out of the Tavistock Clinic in London, began to formulate a new theory of development that recognised the primary influence of the infant–mother relationship on the successful adaptation of the young child. Relying heavily on naturalistic observation, but also drawing on the results of empirical studies, Bowlby developed what we now know as 'Attachment Theory'.

Amongst his research associates at the Tavistock Clinic in the early 1950s was a woman called Mary Ainsworth. Her prior interest was in 'security theory', which proposed that infants and young children need to develop a secure dependence on their parents before launching out into unfamiliar situations. Through observational studies of mothers and their infants in Uganda and the United States, and her later studies using an experiment called 'the strange situation' (which is discussed later in the chapter),[4] Ainsworth made a significant contribution to the classification of different types of attachment, and the identification of the pivotal contribution of the mother's sensitivity to her infant in the development of attachment patterns.

WHAT IS THE ROLE OF ATTACHMENT?

Central to Attachment Theory is the concept of there being a survival advantage for the infant associated with maintaining closeness to adults and, thus, protection and accessibility to needs-provision. Because the emotional tie the infant forms with his or her caregivers has aided survival of the species, early Attachment Theorists considered that this characteristic of human activity has been selected through evolutionary processes.

According to Attachment Theorists, attachment relationships play a key role in:

- the young child's development
- their perception of relatedness with others
- their concept of self, and
- their life experiences.

We will now look at each of these in turn.

The young child's development

Development unfolds in a use-dependent manner: that is, the young child learns about important aspects of their physical, emotional and social worlds, and masters various developmental tasks (e.g. crawling, walking, grasping, talking, playing, socialising), through experience, exploration and play. Experience, exploration and play are directly influenced by the extent to which the child feels safe and secure. Feelings of safety and security are directly influenced by the quality of the attachment the child experiences with their primary caregiver(s).

Consider three infants aged one year. One is developing what is called a '*secure* attachment' to his caregivers; the other two infants are what is called '*insecure*'. The secure infant will move away from his caregiver in order to explore his physical and social world. From time to time he will resume close proximity to his caregiver before moving away again. Increasingly, he will merely orient visually to his caregiver and vocalise to her. All the while he is exploring and experiencing his physical, emotional and social world. His motor and cognitive development is stimulated through play. His social and language development is stimulated through interactions with others. His emotional development is stimulated through shared emotional experiences.

In contrast, one of the insecure infants is clingy and obsessed with the parent, and the other appears disengaged from the parent and others. One seeks to be held all the time and protests at being placed on the floor. He is fearful and requires constant reassurance. His preoccupation with safety and the accessibility and responsiveness of his caregiver (arising from inconsistent care) limits his experiences, his exploration and his play and, hence, all aspects of his development. The other infant has apparently learnt that adults are consistently undependable and that interacting with them is a pointless, distressing, and even a frightening activity. Though appearing disinterested, he is likely to be highly fearful as he perceives that he must take care of himself in a world that is uncaring and potentially unsafe. His fearfulness reduces the likelihood of exploration, thereby also impacting adversely on all aspects of his development and his emotional well-being.

The child's perception of relatedness with others

In addition, it is within the context of the primary attachment relationships that young children learn about being in a relationship with another human being, where primary attachment relationships constitute the attachment relationships the child has with his or her primary caregiver. Children develop a sense of trust in others as a result of parental accessibility and sensitive responsiveness to their child's needs. Importantly, through the experience of emotional connectedness with the primary caregiver, children explore and integrate a range of emotions, and through shared emotional experiences develop the foundations of a capacity for empathy. Through their efforts to please their caregivers and to avoid displeasing them, children internalise (that is, understand and accept) social rules and learn to restrict their impulses to engage in seriously aberrant behaviour (i.e. behaviour that is not socially accepted and that compromises the quality of the child's interactions with others) and extreme displays of negative affect (affect meaning emotion). Children's behaviour and affect become regulated by a concern for maintaining positive and loving relationships with their caregivers, thus establishing the foundations for a life of lawfulness, positive relationships with others and successful parenting of their own children.

The child's concept of self

The nature of a child's attachment and attachment relationships will contribute to their concept of self. In association with care that is consistent, sensitive and encouraging of their efforts, the infant perceives him- or herself to be good, lovable and competent.

The child's life experiences

Finally, attachment relationships play an important role throughout the life-span. In the context of a strong, secure and trusting relationship with another, a person is likely to feel empowered to take risks, accept challenges and cope with failure. Hence, a strong and secure attachment relationship facilitates the ability to enjoy full and satisfying life experiences throughout the life-span.

HOW DOES ATTACHMENT DEVELOP?

An infant is not born with attachments already made to its primary caregivers. This special relationship emerges over time and through a series of stages. Perhaps the most common model of attachment development, based on the work of John Bowlby[5,6] and Mary Ainsworth (and associates),[7] and summarised by Richard Delaney,[8] is the one illustrated in Table 1.1.

WHAT DOES ATTACHMENT LOOK LIKE?

John Bowlby referred to 'attachment behaviour' as any form of activity that results in a child accessing and/or maintaining proximity to some other clearly identified individual who the child believes is better able to cope with the world. It is most obvious whenever the child is frightened, fatigued, or sick, and is relieved by comforting and caregiving. At other times the behaviour is less in evidence. Nevertheless, the knowledge that an attachment figure is accessible and responsive provides a strong and pervasive feeling of security, and so encourages the child to value and continue the relationship. Whilst attachment behaviour is at its most obvious in early childhood, it can be observed throughout the life-span, especially in emergencies.[9]

Attachment behaviours provide an insight into the nature of a child's attachment relationships. They serve to keep the caregiver connected to the child physically ('My caregiver is nearby'), emotionally ('My caregiver understands my feelings') and cognitively ('My caregiver is aware of me'). In children these behaviours include:[10]

- eye-to-eye gaze
- reaching
- smiling
- signalling or calling to

- pouting
- holding or clinging
- protesting separation
- seeking to be picked up
- following
- sitting with
- searching
- verbal engagement/need expression.

WHAT DIFFERENT TYPES OF ATTACHMENT EXIST?

Attachment patterns were formalised using a procedure known as the Strange Situation.[11] In this procedure the mother and twelve-month-old child are introduced to a laboratory play room. An unfamiliar adult joins them shortly thereafter. While the stranger plays with the baby the mother leaves briefly and then returns. A second separation occurs, during which the baby is left completely alone. Finally, the stranger and then the mother return. The whole procedure takes approximately twenty minutes. The baby's interaction with mother and stranger, and its reaction to separations and reunions, were studied in order to formulate the following attachment patterns:

- secure
- insecure–avoidant
- insecure–ambivalent
- disorganised/disoriented.

We will now look at each of these in more detail.

Table 1.1 Stages of attachment formation

Stage	Time	Observable features
Pre-attachment	Birth to 3 months	The infant orients to the sound of the caregiver's voice, reflexively reaches to be held, tracks the caregiver visually, but smiles reflexively and indiscriminately.
Recognition/ discrimination	3–8 months	The infant begins to differentiate between their primary caregivers and others. Smiles are based on recognition, and the infant scans the caregivers' faces with excitement. The infant shows distress when caregivers leave the room and smiles at and greets them after brief separations.
Active attachment	8–36 months	During this stage in which the primary attachments are actively developing, the infant demonstrates a clear preference for the primary caregiver or caregivers and a corresponding wariness towards strangers, or 'stranger reaction'. The infant crawls or walks away from their caregivers to explore their environment, though they frequently check back to their caregiver's face, either by returning to their caregiver or visually touching base with him or her. The child explores without anxiety. Once mobile, the child seeks hugs and otherwise seeks temporary reunions with their caregiver before resuming their exploration of their environment. Such temporary reunions are referred to as 'emotional refuelling'.
Partnership	36 months onwards	In this stage attachment solidifies. The child expresses their needs verbally and begins to negotiate conflicts and differences with their caregiver.

Securely attached infants and children

Securely attached infants[12] and children exhibit a preference for contact and involvement with their primary caregiver, though after an initial period of shyness ('stranger reaction') will feel comfortable enough to engage with strangers towards whom their caregiver shows no anxiety. Similarly, the child will be content to explore an unfamiliar setting without apparent anxiety (i.e. unreasonable fear) in the presence of their caregiver. As they develop a sense of 'basic trust' (or perception that the world is a safe place and that relating to others is a satisfying experience) they are content to be left alone with a relative stranger for a short period of time. They exhibit excitement at their caregiver's return and will top-up their emotional cup by initiating a temporary reunion, such as sharing a brief hug, before resuming their confident exploration of their physical and social world. Although estimates vary, research in Western countries has shown that around 60 per cent of 12–20-month-old infants studied using the Strange Situation might be classified as evidencing an emerging 'secure attachment'.

Insecure–avoidant infants and children

Insecure–avoidant infants[13] and children appear on the surface to cope best with separations from their primary caregiver. Lacking a strong emotional connection to their primary caregiver, they will exhibit no clear preference for their caregiver or a relative stranger. Rather, they appear relatively detached and self-reliant, even self-absorbed. They may avoid or ignore others and rarely initiate affectionate gestures. In their caregiver's embrace, they are likely to be observed to orient their face away from the caregiver and fail to cling or return an embrace. As children, they are more likely to prefer solitary activities and might be described as 'loners'. They appear to have learnt that relating to others is an unsatisfying experience – such as might occur in cases where a caregiver is typically unresponsive due to being absent, having poor parenting skills or as a result of their own avoidant pattern of relating.

Insecure–ambivalent infants and children

Insecure–ambivalent infants[14] are excessively clingy towards their caregiver and distressed during separation. Upon reunion with their caregiver they are likely to be inconsolable, obsessed with them, and vacillate between need for closeness with and anger at the caregiver. They are typically difficult for the caregiver to settle and exhibit a mixture of dependency and resistance. Insecure–ambivalent children are perceived to be angry, demanding and needy.

Disorganised/disoriented infants and children

In contrast to the patterns of attachment described above, the defining feature of the disorganised/disoriented infant[15] and child is that they exhibit no consistent or organised attachment behaviour in response to reunions with their caregiver. Rather, they display bizarre and contradictory behaviours (such as seeking to be close to their caregiver but with their gaze averted, approaching the caregiver only to stop and stare before full physical reunion occurs, and alternately, engaging with and disengaging from their caregiver almost simultaneously), and exhibit incomplete movements and affective displays (such as reaching to be held or starting to protest only to freeze and/or engage in dazed-like behaviour). In addition, disorganised/disoriented infants exhibit signs of worry in the presence of their caregiver, such that they might sit on the caregiver's lap but with eyes averted, or might allow the caregiver to hold them but with their limbs stiff. They might also be observed to avoid or fail to seek out their caregiver when distressed or frightened and attempt to leave with a stranger rather than their caregiver. It is likely that these infants have experienced trauma in the relationship with their attachment figure and, at the very least, gross deficiencies in needs-provision.

HOW DOES CAREGIVING IMPACT ON ATTACHMENT?

Accessibility and responsiveness

Accessibility to needs-provision is, arguably, the most fundamental drive that influences the behaviour of the infant and young child and their development. Remember the tale of three mice at the beginning of this book. The first mouse experienced reliable and consistent accessibility to needs-provision. As a result, he felt secure in this knowledge and was able to get on with exploring and experiencing other aspects of his physical, emotional and social world.

However, the second mouse and the third mouse experienced problems in accessing needs-provision. The second mouse exhibited features of an insecure–ambivalent attachment, and the third mouse exhibited features of an insecure–avoidant attachment.

'Accessibility' means that the parent is present and available, physically and emotionally, to the infant and child.[16] By parental 'responsiveness' we mean that the caretaker sensitively, accurately and directly addresses the child's needs.[17]

Infants and young children who experience consistent accessibility and responsiveness to needs-provision are able to get on with exploring and learning about their physical, emotional and social worlds. However, infants and young children who experience inconsistent accessibility and responsiveness remain preoccupied with needs-provision and this leaves an indelible mark on their behaviour and adjustment.

Some factors relating to parents and their behaviour that can impact on accessibility and responsiveness are shown in Table 1.2.

Table 1.2 Parenting factors that impact on accessibility and responsiveness

Positive factors	Negative factors
Good parental role models	Parental mental-health problems
Parenting experience	Parental substance abuse
Positive attitude to parenting/ children	Domestic violence
Capacity to identify with others/ empathy	Poor parenting ability/ knowledge
Secure attachment as a child	Insecure attachment as a child

Affective attunement

Another aspect of caregiver behaviour that influences the strength and quality of the primary attachment relationship is 'affective attunement'. Affective attunement is a concept that is used to describe the process whereby the caregiver recognises the emotional expressions of their infant and reflects them back to the infant. When attunement experiences occur, the caregiver seems to experience the same or very similar emotions. This is reflected in research that shows that the heart-rate curves of infants and mothers parallel each other during play.[18] Through affective attunement, the caregiver shares the joy and happiness the infant experiences during play. When the infant is distressed the caregiver also experiences distress. The infant experiences the caregiver's distress in tone of voice and smoothness of movement. Emotional distress is alleviated for both caregiver and infant through the caregiver soothing the infant. The child experiences physical and emotional relaxation in themselves and their caregivers, as does the caregiver. Through repeated attunement experiences the child's emotions are validated and regulated through the responsiveness of the caregiver, thus promoting the child's experience and perception of emotional connectedness with others and facilitating the safe exploration of a range of emotions, emotional self-awareness and, later, a capacity for empathy.

MATTHEW'S STORY

Matthew's case is fictional. It is included here and at the end of each chapter hereafter in order to illustrate important aspects of how attachment disorder develops, what distinguishes it from other childhood mental disorders and normal behaviour in children, and the parenting and treatment requirements of attachment-disordered children. It is not intended to be a benchmark against which all children suspected of having an attachment disorder can be compared. Though it tells the story of a child who has come to the attention of child protection authorities, his presentation, care and intervention requirements are also applicable to adopted children who were initially cared for in institutional-care environments. It should be noted that the presentation of attachment disorder is as varied as the number of children who might be diagnosed with this disorder. No disorder should be diagnosed on the basis of observable behaviour alone. The distinguishing features of attachment-disordered children are that they have a traumatic care history and that their behaviour and affective displays might realistically be seen to reflect exaggerated preoccupations with accessibility to needs-provision, a pessimistic perception of self, other and the world, and anxiety/over-arousal. Though it is written from the perspective of a clinician working with Matthew, it is intended to be reflective of the experiences of child-protection workers, foster and adoptive caregivers and others who are responsible for the care and protection of children like Matthew.

Matthew came to the attention of child-protection authorities when he was five months of age. Police had been repeatedly called out to Matthew's home to respond to domestic disputes. On one occasion they determined that neither parent was in a fit state to care for an infant and child protection authorities were notified. Matthew was removed from the care of his parents and placed in emergency foster-care accommodation. The next day his parents consented to his ongoing temporary placement in foster care while further investigations into his circumstances were conducted. During these investigations it was discovered that Matthew had bruising to his legs and buttocks that appeared to have been inflicted by another person and for which his parents could not offer an adequate explanation. In addition, drug- and alcohol-fuelled domestic violence was identified to be a recurrent feature of the relationship between Matthew's mother and father. Further assessment revealed that both parents had chaotic care histories themselves, limited social support and mental-health problems.

Matthew's initial foster carer reported that Matthew exhibited an exaggerated startle response but cried briefly and rarely. He was not demanding and did not appear to miss his mother and father. He tended to be floppy in the carer's embrace and did not cling. She commented that he was an unusually easy baby to care for, except after family access.

Family access was initially scheduled to occur three times per week for two hours on the erroneous grounds that this was required to preserve the attachment between Matthew and his parents.[19] Matthew was a crowd favourite at the child-protection office. Not only did his blond hair and blue eyes make him cute, he did not appear to mind being passed from staff member to staff member. In fact, he was perceived to be a friendly baby as he appeared to always be gazing at others, no matter which child-protection worker was holding him. However, when Matthew was taken into the access room to meet his parents there was an immediate transformation in his behaviour. He cried when passed from a child-protection worker to either parent. He fretted and was difficult for either parent to settle, though he settled readily when handed back to the access supervisor. While being held by his parents, he maintained an averted gaze, and at times appeared glassy eyed and rigid, particularly when his parents bickered with each other. He became calm again after access and typically fell asleep while being transported back to his foster placement. However, his foster carer reported that he was restless and unsettled for the remainder of the day.

After three months a decision was made that Matthew should remain in foster care for up to twelve months while his parents engaged with services regarding their drug and alcohol misuse, domestic violence, mental-health problems and deficits in their parenting knowledge. Access was reduced to once per week on the grounds that it unsettled Matthew and that there were not the resources to maintain a thrice-weekly access regime anyway. By the time he was twelve months old Matthew had changed placement three times; the first time because the foster carer only provided emergency care; the second time because the foster carer unexpectedly became ill; and a third time because the placement was only intended to be temporary while a suitable longer-term foster carer was identified. His fourth foster carer reported that, at twelve months of age, Matthew remained an unusually easy child to care for, except in the twelve hours after access with his parents. At access times, he was unsettled at separation from his foster carer in order to be transported to the child-protection office, appeared content when being fussed over by child-protection workers at their office, but continued to display unusual behaviours in the presence of his parents. Upon entering the access room at the office he would orient to his parents, smile and begin to move towards them, before stopping, orienting away and seeking to re-engage with the access supervisor. Thereafter, throughout the remainder of each access period it was as if he preferred the access supervisor over his parents. Though he did not protest being held and fussed over by his parents, he continued to orient his face away while on their lap or in their embrace.

CHAPTER SUMMARY

- 'Attachment' is a term used to describe the dependency relationship a child develops towards his or her primary caregivers.

- An 'attachment figure' is defined as someone who provides physical and emotional care, has continuity and consistency in the child's life, and who has an emotional investment in the child's life.[20] A child can have more than one attachment figure (e.g. parents and grandparents), each of whom influence the child's expectations and beliefs about themselves and others. The primary attachment figures, however, are the people who are the main source of needs-provision to the child and the people with whom the child experiences the closest emotional tie.

- Attachment Theory developed in recognition of the importance of the caregiver–infant bond to the development and emotional well-being of the infant.

- Attachment influences the young child's development, their perception of relatedness with others, their concept of self, and their life experiences.

- Attachment develops over time and through a series of stages.

- Caregiving influences quality and type of attachment.

- Quality of attachment influences all aspects of the child's development.

- Parental accessibility (and the child's emerging perceptions regarding parental accessibility) are particularly important to attachment and the child's social, emotional and behavioural functioning and development.

CHAPTER **2**

UNDERSTANDING ATTACHMENT DISORDER

WHAT IS ATTACHMENT DISORDER?

In addition to the patterns of insecure attachment discussed earlier, there is a smaller group of children who might be diagnosed as having an 'attachment disorder'. Formal diagnostic terms for attachment disorder are 'Reactive Attachment Disorder of Infancy or Early Childhood (RAD)' or 'Disinhibited Attachment Disorder (DAD)', depending upon diagnostic conventions in the child's country of origin.

Attachment disorders occur among children who have failed to develop a secure selective attachment to their primary caregiver or caregivers and who have experienced inconsistent, insensitive, inadequate and/or abusive and frightening care. Attachment disorders are characterised by gross disturbance in social and emotional relatedness and behaviour. In association with these disturbances, children with an attachment disorder often exhibit deficits in all aspects of their development. What differentiates attachment disorders from other mental disorders of childhood (e.g. Attention Deficit-Hyperactivity

Disorder – ADHD; Conduct Disorder – CD; Oppositional Defiant Disorder – ODD; Pervasive Developmental Disorder/ Autistic Disorder) is that the above-mentioned disturbances stem from maladaptive perceptions of self, other and world (attachment representations), over-arousal (anxiety), and excessive preoccupation with needs-provision. The other differentiating feature is that these characteristics might reasonably be considered to have arisen in the context of inadequate and/ or abusive care.

Many attachment-disordered children show both an avoidance of intimacy and extreme attempts to control close relationships coercively using threatening, angry or menacing behaviours and/or seductive, charming or demanding behaviours. As close relationships for these children have often led to abuse, fear and hurt (shame and rejection), closeness becomes equated with distress or danger and intimacy becomes something to be resisted. The closer a caregiver tries to get to the child or the more love they show, the more threatening they become to the child. Nevertheless, the attachment-disordered child is also uncomfortable with too much distance from the caregiver and associated concern that the caregiver may no longer be under their direct influence. A vicious cycle often ensues, whereby the child draws the caregiver closer through demanding or charming behaviours, only to distance them when they come too close, and then draw the caregiver back in when the distance (physical and/or emotional) becomes too great again. The child's behaviour serves to:

- demand attention and a caregiver response to their needs
- punish and distance the caregiver, and
- release pent-up frustration and anger.

Other attachment-disordered children exhibit diffuse attachments, as manifested by indiscriminate sociability and a marked inability to exhibit appropriate selective attachments.

Such children are typically perceived to be charming and gregarious, are likely to be excessively friendly towards strangers, and do not display appropriate selectivity and orientation towards attachment figures when attachment behaviours are activated (e.g. when hurt, unwell, frightened, hungry).

A third group of attachment-disordered children exhibit both avoidance of intimacy and indiscriminate sociability.

Where care arrangements change (e.g. children in foster or adoptive care), attachment-disordered children often compulsively re-enact their maladaptive interactions with their new caregivers. Like all children, they feel safe and reassured in association with people behaving in predictable and expected ways. As they expect caregivers to be angry and threatening, or undependable and rejecting, they often behave in a manner that precipitates similar behaviour in their new caregivers, thus confirming their belief systems, which is reassuring, and perpetuating the cycle. Their belief systems also tell them that caregivers cannot be trusted or relied upon to understand them and meet their needs. Attachment-disordered children conclude that the only person they can depend upon is themself and the only way to get their needs met is to take matters into their own hands. The outcome is the exhibition of controlling, manipulative behaviours and/or deceptive and deceitful behaviours arising from a preoccupation with accessibility to needs-provision.

The controlling and manipulative behaviours of attachment-disordered children typically take the form of angry, aggressive and destructive behaviours, charming and seductive behaviours or a combination of these. From the first days of life, the infant uses affective displays, such as crying and smiling, to command the attention of their caregivers. Throughout childhood, attachment-disordered children continue to rely on affective displays to assure attention to their needs, punish and distance their caregivers and release pent-up anxiety/arousal.

The attachment-disordered child seeks to communicate

their thoughts, feelings and needs through their behaviour and affective displays, much like a pre-verbal child. In addition to smiling and crying, behaviours and affective displays used to communicate thoughts, feelings and needs might include sulking, tantrums, aggression, destructiveness, clinginess and repetitive actions to secure attention (e.g. turning the TV off, turning lights on and off). As a result of experiencing neglectful care and because of their consequent mistrust of others, these children often do not progress to the stage of articulating their thoughts, feelings, wishes and needs when they acquire the language to do so. They consider controlling, manipulative behaviours and affective displays to be a more effective strategy. When caregivers ignore, admonish or discipline aberrant behaviour and affective displays, the attachment-disordered child feels misunderstood and their belief that their caregivers are uncaring and unresponsive is again confirmed. They see punishment as arbitrary, cruel and rejecting. Their behaviour reflects their expectation of caregiver unavailability, rejection and/or maltreatment, and the imposition of punishment serves to confirm these expectations.

When caregivers learn that love and patience is not enough for these children, they can feel discouraged and reject the child, further contributing to the child's self-concept of being unlovable and their caregivers as rejecting. Caregivers may even develop negative and abusive feelings towards the child. Because these children can be superficially charming to others, especially to those who do not present the threat of intimacy, professionals may see the caregivers as being unduly harsh or rejecting.

Attachment-disordered children demonstrate an apparent lack of concern for maintaining close and loving relationships with their adult caregivers. As a result, compared to other children they are relatively unconcerned about the impact of their behaviour on their relationships with others. Rather, they develop a range of aberrant behaviours that assure accessibility to needs-provision while also punishing and distancing their caregivers. In turn, the caregivers can experience feelings of revulsion and loathing towards the child that impact negatively upon their care of the child and further reinforce the child's negative attributions or beliefs about the relationship. The result, in many cases, where carers lack knowledge and understanding of attachment disorder, is the breakdown of the child's care arrangements, sometimes occurring continually. Unfortunately, this often only serves to reinforce the child's 'negative attachment representations', a subject we look at next.

WHAT ARE ATTACHMENT REPRESENTATIONS?

Attachment representations are the attitudes and beliefs a child develops regarding self, other and their social world. These attitudes and beliefs develop in the context of the infant's primary-attachment relationships and reflect the infant's experience of the accessibility, sensitivity and responsiveness of their primary caregivers. They remain relatively stable over time in the absence of changes in the child's experience of the accessibility, sensitivity and responsiveness of others. Figure 2.1 illustrates attachment representations associated with attachment security and attachment disorder and representations of self and other.

The securely attached child

This child develops a mostly positive attachment representation of themselves, their caregiver, and their world. In association with their experience of accessible, sensitive and responsive care, they perceive themself as being worthwhile/wanted

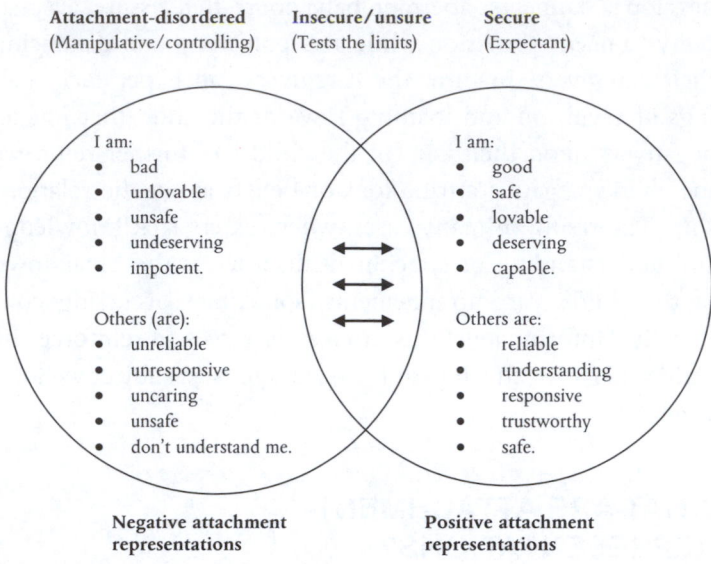

Figure 2.1 Attachment security and representations regarding self and other

('I am loved'), safe ('My caregiver protects me from harmful experiences') and capable ('My caregiver is encouraging and supportive of my efforts').[21] They develop basic trust, an expectation that the world will generally be safe and that close relationships will be satisfying. The securely attached child has a well-formed conscience, a sense of right and wrong that grows out of their desire to please their attachment figures and to avoid displeasing them. The securely attached child attends to their body's cues regarding their needs (e.g. the need for comfort, physical sustenance or to go to the bathroom), a range of genuine emotion, and the ability to identify and express needs through spoken language. Though elements of negative attachment representations are sometimes in evidence, positive attachment representations predominate (see Figure 2.2).

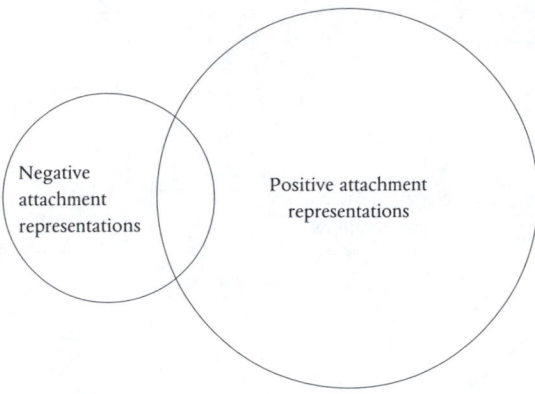

Figure 2.2 Attachment representations of the securely attached child

The attachment-disordered child

In contrast, the attachment representations of attachment-disordered children are essentially negative. In association with rejecting, frightening or abusive care, these children view themselves as worthless ('I am bad and unlovable'), unsafe ('My caregiver will not protected me from traumatic experiences') and impotent ('It is impossible to get my caregiver to respond consistently to my needs').[22, 23] They view their caregivers as being unreliable, unresponsive, rejecting and threatening. They expect intimate relationships to be undependable and ultimately frustrating of their needs.[24] They use manipulation as a means to make their caregivers and others (e.g. teachers) behave in predictable ways in order to promote feelings of security. Though elements of positive attachment representations are sometimes in evidence, negative attachment representations predominate (see Figure 2.3).

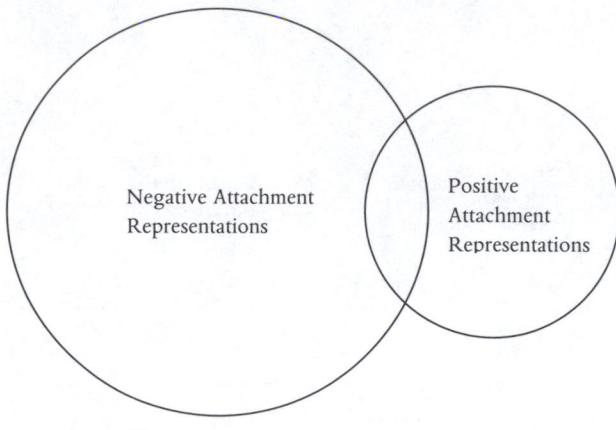

Figure 2.3 Attachment representations of the attachment-disordered child

The insecure child

The attachment representations of insecure children are neither entirely positive nor negative. Rather, they seem to occupy the middle ground, unsure of themselves, others and their place in the world. These children seem to be more likely to engage in testing of the limits of behaviour that will be accepted by a given person (e.g. parent, psychotherapist) or in a given context (e.g. school) rather than coercive or manipulative behaviour. This kind of representation is likely to have arisen in the context of inconsistent parental accessibility and responsiveness, resulting in a child who is perpetually unsure (see Figure 2.4).

Negative attachment representations are thought to develop when normal attachment behaviours consistently fail to elicit sensitive responsiveness from the caregiver, as may occur where there is limited accessibility to a consistent caring adult (e.g. the child lives in an orphanage), where the caregiver lacks basic parenting skills and knowledge, or in cases of parental

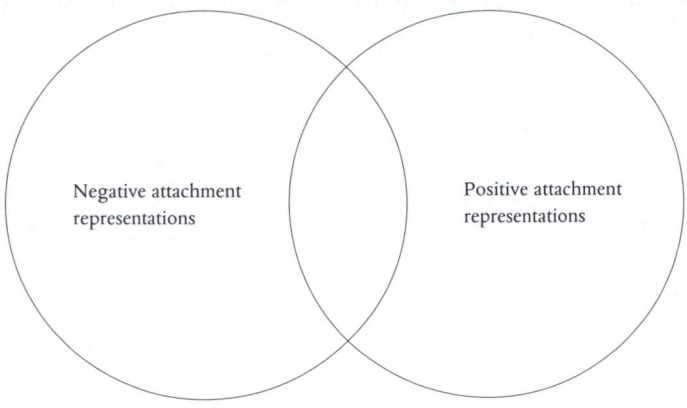

Negative attachment representations

Positive attachment representations

Figure 2.4 Attachment representations of the insecure child

mental disorder, substance abuse or domestic violence. Under these circumstances the infant experiences heightened states of fear and distress, for which they are inconsistently soothed, relaxed or comforted. This frightening state is psychologically unsustainable and young children have to introduce some control into their unpredictable, threatening and uncaring world. They develop the view that the only reliable element is themself, and that the only way to feel remotely safe and to get one's needs met is to take control (i.e. 'It is a dog-eat-dog world. The only person you can rely on is yourself...').

WHAT IS THE CONTRIBUTION OF AROUSAL AND OVER-AROUSAL?

Attachment-disordered children are often chronically overaroused in association with having been traumatised and inconsistently soothed in their primary-dependency relationships (that is, their relationship(s) with the person or persons who cared for them as small infants). This leaves them susceptible to anxiety and associated problems with learning, affect regulation (i.e. the ability to control the intensity of one's emotions) and behavioural control.

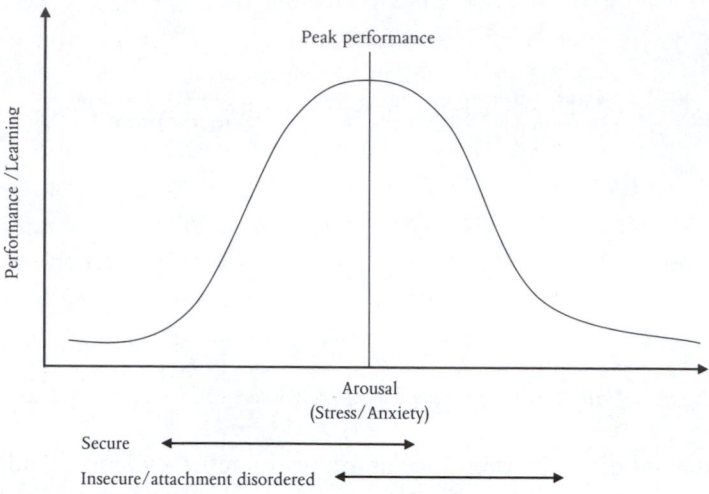

Figure 2.5 Relationship between arousal and performance/learning

Figure 2.5 illustrates the relationship between stress/arousal and performance/learning. A certain degree of arousal (i.e. brain activity, alertness, attention) is necessary for peak performance and learning. However, there is a threshold beyond which performance and learning decline in association with increases in stress and arousal. This is best illustrated by the example of walking a balance beam. Most people can successfully negotiate their way across a balance beam raised off the ground by a house brick at each end. They consider themselves able and have no concerns for their physical safety. However, place the same balance beam between the windows of two adjacent buildings ten storeys off the ground and most people would experience heightened states of anxiety/over-arousal. They would be overwhelmed by fear regarding their physical safety. They would doubt their ability to negotiate the balance beam successfully. They would lose coordination and their performance would suffer accordingly, thus confirming their fear that they will be harmed and exacerbating their anxiety/over-arousal. In association with their own chronically over-aroused state, the performance and learning of attachment-disordered children is similarly compromised.

Figure 2.6 illustrates how the chronically over-aroused state experienced by attachment-disordered children impacts adversely on their behaviour and emotions. In contrast to securely attached children, whose normal states of arousal rarely reach the so-called 'threshold to madness', or 'anxiety threshold', beyond which the organism has to release pent-up anxiety or suffer negative physical and emotional consequences, the chronically over-aroused, attachment-disordered child exists much closer to this threshold. Stimuli and events that have a comparatively minor impact on the secure child can much more readily push the attachment-disordered child past the 'threshold to madness', whereupon they seek to reduce arousal through aggressive and destructive behaviours (fight), hyperactive behaviour (flight) and/or dissociative behaviours (freeze). Dissociation is a psychological defence whereby the mind switches off or goes elsewhere in response to extreme anxiety and trauma. The flight/fight/freeze response to heightened levels of anxiety/over-arousal is considered to have been naturally selected through evolution in order to achieve safety and well-being in the face of threats to the organism, much as attachment is thought to have developed through evolutionary processes. Seen in this way, aggressive, destructive, hyperactive and disengaged behaviours exhibited by attachment-disordered children are a necessary response to over-arousal as the purpose of such behaviour is to neutralise a perceived threat. They should be met with understanding, empathy and other measures to assist the child to reduce arousal as opposed to anger and discipline alone – the latter only serving to perpetuate the child's unsustainable levels of over-arousal and associated fight/flight/freeze response. Hence, arousal management is a key aspect to the care and management of attachment-disordered children.

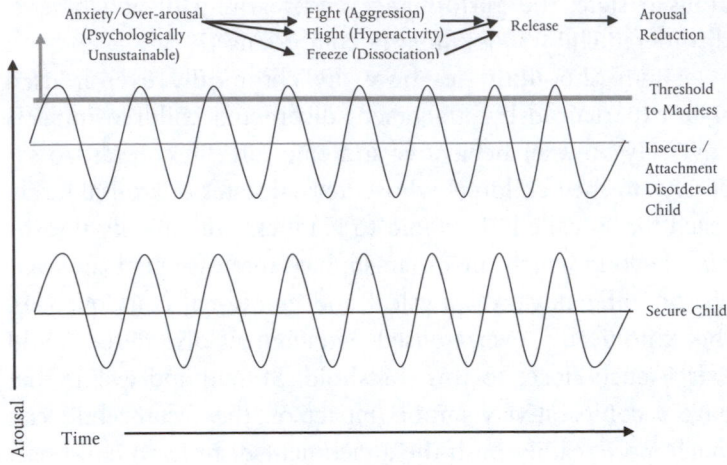

Figure 2.6 Patterns of arousal and over-arousal

In addition, in association with their chronic high arousal and anxiety levels, attachment-disordered children tend to be hypervigilant to (that is, constantly on the lookout for, and highly aware of) stimuli in their environment that have previously been associated with actual or perceived threat and hyperreactive to such stimuli. They appear to their caregivers to 'make mountains out of molehills'. They are more prone than other children to aggressive, destructive, hyperactive and dissociative (going away in the mind, switching off from what is happening, where what is happening is too stressful or frightening for the child to cope with) behaviours, the purpose of each being to lower arousal and release anxiety, thereby engendering feelings of well-being. Children who behave like this are often misdiagnosed with Attention Deficit Hyperactivity Disorder (ADHD), Conduct Disorder and Oppositional Defiant Disorder (ODD).

The consequences of misdiagnosis is that attachment-disordered children may receive treatment that is at best benign, and at worse counter-productive. Take the example of an attachment-disordered child being diagnosed with ADHD. This occurs commonly as both disorders are generally diagnosed on the basis of observable behaviours attributed to each disorder, which overlap. Overlapping behaviours include difficulties with behavioural control (impulsivity, hyperactivity, aggression, destructiveness) and with maintaining attention.

The most commonly utilised treatment for ADHD is stimulant medication (e.g. Ritalin, Dexamphetamine). This is because it is assumed that the brain of the ADHD child is *under*-aroused. This would explain their inattentive behaviour and difficulty concentrating for long periods. It is further assumed that these children engage in hyperactive behaviour as a means of stimulating brain activity and increasing arousal to normal levels. Hence, stimulant medication produces a so-called 'paradoxical effect', in that it calms the ADHD child's behaviour by chemically elevating brain activity and arousal levels, thereby taking away the need for hyperactivity. It also leads to improved attention and concentration in the truly ADHD child.

On the other hand, the attachment-disordered child can often be disengaged from, and inattentive towards, others in the context of their inability to form meaningful relationships. These children struggle with attention and concentration due to high arousal/anxiety levels. They dissociate. Attachment-disordered children exhibit apparent difficulties with behavioural control (impulsivity, hyperactivity, aggression, destructiveness) as a function of their need to 'blow off steam', control others, and reduce arousal/anxiety levels. Prescription of stimulant medications conceivably maintains high arousal levels and, hence, the perceived problematic behaviour. Where any positive effect is noticed, such as reduced motor activity, reduced aggression and reduced hostility, it is possible that this is a function of induced dissociation resulting in reduced motor activity. More commonly, attachment-disordered children are concurrently prescribed medications that lower arousal (e.g. Catapres/Clonidine). Effects are mixed depending on relative doses and what static point in arousal is achieved. Where medication is offered, medications that lower arousal are more likely to be effective for attachment-disordered children; medication that increases arousal possibly being more effective for truly ADHD children. Children are unlikely to be appropriately diagnosed with both disorders. Caution should be exercised when withdrawing attachment-disordered children from stimulant medication due to the possibility of the combined effect of arousal-reducing medication and the brain's own corrective measures pushing arousal too low, possibly artificially/chemically inducing an attention-deficit disorder. Figure 2.7 illustrates the relative effects of medication regimes in the treatment of ADHD and attachment-disordered children.

WHAT IS THE SIGNIFICANCE OF PARENTAL ACCESSIBILITY?

In the 1930s, experimental psychologist B.F. Skinner developed an apparatus to study learning behaviour in laboratory animals. Referred to as the 'Skinner Box', this box-like apparatus incorporated a lever or bar, and a food chute. Rats were placed in the Skinner Box and exposed to three 'learning conditions'.

- In the first condition, a pellet of food was delivered via the chute each time the rat pressed the bar or lever. This condition was referred to as 'continuous reinforcement'. The rats quickly learnt that by pressing the bar or lever they would receive food.

- In the second condition, a food pellet was delivered randomly, such as on the first, fifth, eighth, or thirteenth press of the bar or lever. This condition was referred to as 'intermittent reinforcement'. The rats learnt more slowly that by pressing the bar food would be delivered.

- In the third condition no food was delivered through the chute, no matter how many times the rat pressed the bar or lever.

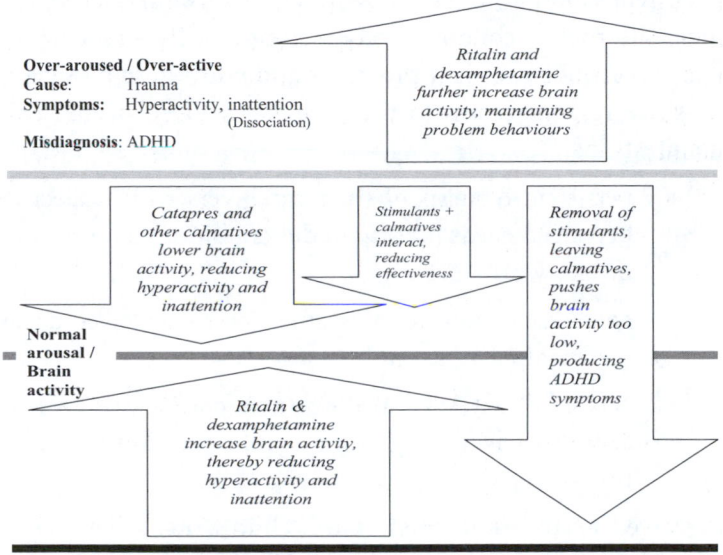

Over-aroused / Over-active
Cause: Trauma
Symptoms: Hyperactivity, inattention
(Dissociation)
Misdiagnosis: ADHD

Ritalin and dexamphetamine further increase brain activity, maintaining problem behaviours

Catapres and other calmatives lower brain activity, reducing hyperactivity and inattention

Stimulants + calmatives interact, reducing effectiveness

Removal of stimulants, leaving calmatives, pushes brain activity too low, producing ADHD symptoms

Normal arousal / Brain activity

Ritalin & dexamphetamine increase brain activity, thereby reducing hyperactivity and inattention

Under-aroused / under-active
Cause: Unknown
Symptoms: Hyperactivity (self-correction), inattention
Diagnosis: ADHD

Figure 2.7 Relative effects of medication regimes in the treatment of ADHD and attachment-disordered children

The rats in the first condition appeared to press the bar or lever when they required food. The rats in the third condition soon stopped pressing the bar. The rats in the second condition pressed the bar persistently, even after food was no longer delivered in association with presses of the bar or lever.

Attachment disorder arises in the context of parental care that reflects conditions two and three referred to above; that is, parental care that involves inconsistent needs-provision or a persistent failure to offer needs-provision. As a result, attachment-disordered children become inordinately preoccupied with accessibility to their providers and with those providers' sensitive responsiveness to the child's perceived needs. This manifests in:

- persistent requests of their caregivers with respect to perceived needs (arising under conditions akin to condition two)

- coercive attempts to draw attention to perceived needs (i.e. manipulation), and

- acts of deceit (e.g. stealing) to secure access to perceived needs (arising under conditions akin to condition three).

Perceived needs are defined as the child's own appraisal of what they require at a given time. They may reflect actual, current needs, such as the need for food, drink, clothing, shelter, assistance and protection. However, among attachment-disordered children, perceived needs often reflect needs that, historically, were unmet and/or inconsistently responded to, under conditions where parental care was deficient or inconsistent. Deficient or inconsistent parental care can arise in association with:

- failure of the parent to bond to the infant/child

- institutional care environments where there is a large ratio of children to adults and children are left

> unsoothed and not responded to for protracted periods of time, and

- parental mental-health problems, substance misuse, domestic disturbance, illness and incapacity.

Take food, for example. Attachment-disordered children are often preoccupied with accessibility to food, make frequent requests for food even when full, will gorge themself until they are sick if allowed unrestricted access to large amounts of food, and will steal food. All of this occurs regardless of whether or not they are hungry and whether or not they receive adequate food. In these children, although they may complain of being hungry (and may actually experience greater desire for food in association with faster metabolism, stemming from early denial of required nourishment) their obsession with food is likely to reflect enduring concern regarding accessibility to this most basic need and the sensitive responsiveness of others to this need.

A further consequence of inconsistent and inadequate needs-provision is that many attachment-disordered children fail to develop a clear idea of how to consistently and successfully access needs-provision in a socially accepted way (e.g. by asking). Rather, they throw at their caregivers a diverse range of behaviours and affective displays in the frantic hope that one of these might elicit needs-provision, or secure access to needs-provision via manipulation or deceit. The failure to develop and demonstrate consistent, successful and socially sanctioned strategies to access needs-provision is most obvious among children whose early attachments might be classified as 'disorganised'. Disorganised attachment behaviour becomes self-reinforcing as adults fail to understand it, feel overwhelmed by it, and institute behavioural sanctions in response to behaviour that is perceived by them as aberrant and/or age-inappropriate – notwithstanding the fact that it was the child's only manner of signalling that they required a response to a perceived need.

The inability to access needs-provision consistently and successfully reinforces the attachment-disordered child's perception of the world and others as harsh and uncaring, and of themselves as bad, unlovable and powerless. This promotes anxiety and maintains heightened arousal levels, which, in turn, results in problems of emotional and behavioural control. The attachment-disordered child requires verbalisation of understanding regarding what their behaviour represents and a response to the need as well as the behaviour. (Examples of such verbalisation appear later in this book.) In addition, the attachment-disordered child requires assistance to develop clear, consistent, successful and socially sanctioned strategies to access needs-provision.

Finally, during the first year of life infants are developing an understanding and appreciation of 'object constancy' and 'object permanency'. In the early part of the first year, infants appear to believe that the only things that exist are what they can see, hear, smell, touch or taste at that moment. When something is removed from their sensory experience, it is as if it ceases to exist; hence the five-month-old's distress when their parent walks out of the room. However, during the latter half of the first year infants are acquiring the capacity to recognise familiar persons and objects as unchanging (object constancy). The ability to perceive objects and persons as unchanging conceivably is reassuring to the infant as it represents an emerging capacity to perceive their world as consistent and predictable. In addition, during the second year and in association with ongoing cognitive development and continued sensitive and responsive care, infants acquire the capacity to develop and hold a mental representation of their understanding, accessible and responsive parent (or object), even at times when the parent (or object) is not physically present ('object permanency'). This is a source of immense comfort and reassurance to the infant and allows them to explore their physical world without anxiety and promotes their tolerance of separations.

In contrast, in association with an unstable and otherwise deficient care environment that impairs normal learning and development during the first two years, attachment-disordered children appear to have failed to acquire an understanding of the constancy of objects and persons, or their permanence. As a result, attachment-disordered children compulsively seek to control all aspects of the person or object, including proximity to it, in an endeavour to reassure themselves regarding their accessibility to desired objects and caregivers and their constancy/predictability. The result is a degree of obsessionality with objects and caregivers that continues to interfere with much, if not all, aspects of their daily lives.

HOW DO I KNOW IF A CHILD HAS AN ATTACHMENT DISORDER?

Not all children who display emotional and behavioural problems warrant clinical diagnosis with a disorder such as Reactive Attachment Disorder (RAD) or Disinhibited Attachment Disorder (DAD). In fact, most problematic behaviours and affective displays are exhibited by all children at least some of the time. That is, normality and abnormality generally are not determined by the presence or absence of problematic behaviours and affective displays. Rather, normality and abnormality are differentiated *by frequency and intensity* of problematic behaviours and affective displays.

In addition, diagnosis on the basis of observable behaviour and affective displays is fraught with difficulties. As has been covered, an over-aroused child exhibits similar behaviour and affective displays as an under-aroused child. Both might attract a range of possible diagnoses, including Reactive Attachment Disorder (RAD), Oppositional Defiant

Disorder (ODD), Conduct Disorder (CD), Attention Deficit Hyperactivity Disorder (ADHD), Asperger's Syndrome, and so on. As mentioned earlier, getting the diagnosis right has implications for treatment, as what works for one diagnosis may not be effective or appropriate in the case of another diagnosis.

In order to determine whether a child with whom one is involved may have an attachment disorder, one needs to consider all the following: historical factors, biological factors, developmental factors and emotional/behavioural/attitudinal factors. The child must also report or otherwise exhibit evidence of negative attachment representations, such as might be reflected in the belief that it is a harsh world, that people do not understand or care, that the only person you can rely on is yourself, and that they are characteristically bad.

We will now look at each of these factors in a bit more detail.

Historical factors

With regard to these, a child might only be diagnosed with an attachment disorder if they have a history of inadequate and/or traumatic care in the first four years of life. This can include the sudden loss of a parent or parents, sudden changes in involvement with a parent or parents, abuse and/or neglect by a parent or parents, exposure to domestic violence, drug and alcohol abuse and mental-health problems by parents that impairs their parental accessibility and responsiveness, and recurrent illnesses (such as reflux, colic, ear infections and tonsillitis) that result in difficulties for the parent(s) in being able to consistently soothe the child and relieve their distress.

Biological and developmental factors

The most obvious biological factor is over-arousal stemming from exposure to trauma and inconsistent or inadequate soothing, such as might occur in each of the scenarios referred to above. Over-arousal manifests in high reactivity to external stimulation (e.g. noise), low frustration tolerance, sleeping difficulties, hyperactivity and poor emotional and behavioural control. The main developmental factor is failure to regulate one's own emotions and have the capacity to self-soothe. In association with high arousal/anxiety levels and associated impairment in performance and learning, attachment-disordered children often exhibit specific or generalised developmental delays or deficits.

Emotional/behavioural/attitudinal factors

In addition to noting if the child displays emotional, behavioural and attitudinal problems frequently and intensively, one needs to be able to establish whether the child about whom a diagnosis of attachment disorder is being considered exhibits maladjustment in order to release anxiety and manipulate their environment and the people within it so as to ensure accessibility to needs-provision, while also punishing and distancing those who have or who might cause them emotional pain. For example, it is not sufficient that the child frequently lies about wrongdoings. One must be convinced that the child frequently lies about wrongdoings because they see relationships as extremely tenuous and lies so as to not threaten accessibility to needs-provision.

WHAT DOES ATTACHMENT DISORDER LOOK LIKE?

Attachment-disordered children exhibit some, or all, of the characteristics presented in Table 2.1 more frequently and with greater intensity than one might normally expect from a same-aged child.

Table 2.1 Characteristics of attachment-disordered children

Characteristic	Manifestations
Maladaptive perception of self	Poor self-concept Poor self-care Bodily function disturbances (e.g. wetting, soiling) Low expectations of deservedness
Maladaptive perception of other	Avoidance of engagement/intimacy Lack of empathy Habitual mistrust Superficial charm
Maladaptive perception of the social world	Preoccupation with safety Preoccupation with fairness Preoccupation with rules Preoccupation with consistency Preoccupation with knowing[1]
Over-arousal (Anxiety)	Aggression Hyperactivity Destructiveness Inattention Dissociation Emotional lability (Instability) Developmental/Learning problems/delays Watchfulness/Hypervigilance
Preoccupation with accessibility to needs-provision	Controlling Demanding Manipulative Charming Deceitful

1 'Preoccupation with knowing' refers to the attachment-disordered child's tendency to ask repetitive questions about arrangements for their care and needs-provision, such as wanting to know where their caregiver will be while they are at school, who will collect them from school, when they will be collected from school, how their caregiver will know when to collect them, and so on

MATTHEW'S STORY (CONTINUED)

Matthew was referred to a psychotherapist when he was six years old. By that time he was being repeatedly suspended from school and his latest foster placement was at breaking point. In his initial interview with the psychotherapist, Matthew was friendly but watchful. Almost immediately he sought to sit in the psychotherapist's high-backed chair and play on the psychotherapist's computer. He was compliant when directed but resistant when asked. He was scruffy and smelled of urine and of having soiled himself. On a number of occasions during the interview he asked where his foster carer was and sought to check on her whereabouts. He expressed an ambivalent perception of school. He identified it as a place where games were played but lamented the fact that there were so many rules. He complained that his teacher shouted too much and that his peers bullied him. He grandiosely claimed that he was good at 'everything' and not so good at 'nothing'. He asserted that he made himself happy and no one made him angry, sad or scared, or hurt him or his feelings. He confidently claimed that he looked after himself when he was unwell, that he 'let it bleed' when he was hurt, and that he wanted 'nobody' to cuddle him when sad or protect him when scared.

At her own interview Matthew's foster carer, his fifth, reported that Matthew demanded her attention and followed her around 'constantly', even to the toilet. She complained that his stomach was a 'bottomless pit' and that stealing food was a problem at home and school. She reported that he was a poor sleeper, often laying awake until midnight and appearing to go 'ten rounds with Mike Tyson' while he slept. She expressed a belief that he would sleep with her in her bed if she allowed him to. She suspected that he roamed the house, taking food and other items, while she slept. She considered that he used anger as a tool to intimidate and manipulate people, though she recalled incidents where his angry outbursts became so intense and so prolonged that he appeared zoned out and no longer connected with his surroundings. She added that extreme tantrums could be precipitated by the slightest provocation, such as asking him to put his shoes in his room. She acknowledged that he did not like being told what to do and preferred to be the boss. She perceived that despite his bravado he was a frightened little boy at heart, being reluctant to leave the home and having a tendency to give up easily when confronted with new experiences. She considered that this was behind much of his problems at school, which included oppositional and defiant behaviours towards teaching staff and controlling and aggressive behaviours towards his peers. She claimed that caring for Matthew was like being on an emotional rollercoaster, and she acknowledged feeling harassed and defeated.

More generally, Matthew's foster carer reported that Matthew received speech therapy for immature articulation of sounds in words. She understood that the delays in his speech stemmed from a suspected history of recurrent ear infections. She recalled that his suspected history of ear infections and associated hearing problems were only realised in association with investigations into his immature speech some months after he entered her care as a three-year-old. She confirmed that Matthew had entered her care in association with his previous placement breaking down due to his foster carer having reported to child-protection authorities that she was unable to cope with Matthew's increasingly demanding behaviour and tantrums.

CHAPTER SUMMARY

- Attachment-disordered children are differentiated from other children by their:

- o excessive preoccupation with accessibility to needs-provision
- o negative perceptions and expectations regarding self and other (negative attachment representations)
- o over-aroused brain.

- One cannot diagnose on the basis of observable behaviour and affective displays alone. One must identify the *reason for* the behaviour. In attachment-disordered children, the reason must relate to one or more of the above.

CHAPTER 3

PARENTING THE ATTACHMENT-DISORDERED CHILD

THE IMPORTANCE OF PROMOTING STRONG AND SECURE ATTACHMENT RELATIONSHIPS

Normally developing children respect and value the relationships they have with their caregivers and other significant people in their lives. They learn to regulate (i.e. control) their behaviour out of a concern for maintaining close and loving relationships with these people and in order to avoid feelings of shame. In doing so, they become knowledgeable about acceptable standards of behaviour at home and in the community and conform to these. In short, they become 'socialised'.

The behaviour of attachment-disordered children is not as strongly regulated by such social forces. Where they perceive themselves to be bad, unloved, undeserving and uncared for, and adults as insensitive, unreliable, uncaring and unresponsive, they can become preoccupied with securing needs-provision at whatever cost. They are therefore less likely to regulate their behaviour out of concern for maintaining positive and loving relationships with others. They may not have a relationship with anyone in their life whom they respect and value sufficiently for the relationship to be a powerful regulating influence over their behaviour. They are prone to unregulated, anti-social behaviour and affective displays, for which they experience little guilt or remorse.

Figure 3.1 illustrates the relationship between attachment, social integration and behaviour. Essentially, secure attachment representations predispose a child/person to making and maintaining quality relationships with family, friends and others in their social network. Secure individuals are integrated into a social world and largely conform to the moral and ethical values and standards of behaviour of their network. Their network tends to be consistent with broader moral and ethical values and conventional standards of behaviour in society as secure individuals are, by definition, well adjusted. In contrast, attachment-disordered individuals are less integrated into mainstream society. As a result, they are less likely to conform to conventional standards of behaviour. Though they may form their own social networks, these are most likely to be comprised of similarly maladjusted individuals whose moral

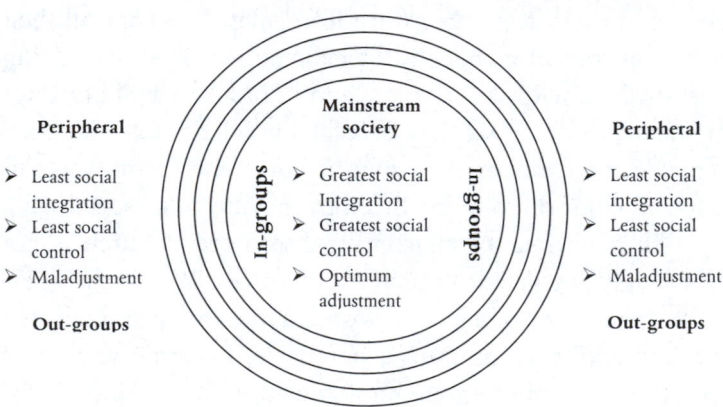

Figure 3.1 The relationship between attachment, social integration and behaviour

and ethical values and standards of behaviour are deviant (e.g. paedophile networks). They are more likely to commit anti-social and unconscionable acts in the pursuit of securing needs-provision. Thus, it can be seen that the resolution of an individual's attachment problems is likely to benefit the whole community as well as that individual.

FIRST PRINCIPLES

When considering what form parental care for the attachment-disordered child must take, it is helpful to consider the conditions under which secure primary-attachment relationships develop. When children are born they are totally dependent on adults to care for and protect them. They are innately endowed with the capacity to call attention to their fundamental needs, but do not have the capacity to satisfy their needs themselves. They rely on adults to do so. They also rely on adults to make all the necessary decisions and take such action as keeps them safe from harm and promotes their development. During the second year of life and in association with the infant's capacity to move, the caring adult supervises them closely and maintains clear and consistent boundaries to keep them safe from harm. In addition, throughout the child's infancy the caring adult demonstrates an awareness of the importance of maintaining stability and consistency of routines in order to facilitate a functional understanding of how one lives one's life. The maintenance of routines is a source of comfort and reassurance to the child as it facilitates an understanding of the predictability of events and the behaviour and responsiveness of others.

When they are cared for by adults who consistently and accurately attend to their physical and emotional needs, infants develop a perception that adults are accessible, concerned about them, understand, and can be relied upon to respond to their needs sensitively. Similarly, in association with their experience of adults making decisions and taking action to keep them safe from harm and promote their development, children develop a perception that their caregivers care about them. These perceptions and beliefs allow the child to confidently go forth into the world, exploring and accepting challenges without inordinate fear of failure, such that all aspects of their development and adjustment are then promoted.

By 'first principles' it is meant that the caregivers of attachment-disordered children should provide the kind of structured, understanding, responsive and regulated care environment that supports and nurtures the development of secure attachment relationships in young children and facilitates their positive socialisation. In practice, attachment-disordered children are typically directed rather than asked with respect to caregiver expectations concerning their behaviour, have most decisions regarding their care and well-being made for them by their caregivers, but have opportunities to experience adults as understanding, interested, responsive and fun. Importantly, caregivers of attachment-disordered children need to be authoritative, which means that they have to set and maintain clear and consistent boundaries and avoid fighting battles with the child that they may ultimately lose, such as the daily battle to get the child to place dirty dishes in the dishwasher. To regularly and repeatedly lose battles with a child weakens the adult and increases the child's insecurity and associated maladjustment.

Finally, the most important achievements of the first two years of any infant's life (which are particularly important goals in the care of an attachment-disordered child) are the development of a positive sense of self, other and the world (secure attachment representations) and the capacity to self-regulate emotion and arousal. These achievements arise in association with the infant's experience and perception that adults are accessible, understanding and responsive to their needs. All other developmental achievements (e.g. bladder and bowel control; pro-social behaviour) follow on from these achievements. Hence, reassuring the child about caregiver accessibility and responsiveness is the first principle in caring for the attachment-disordered child.

ADDRESSING ACCESSIBILITY PREOCCUPATIONS

The ability to gain access to needs-provision is a source of comfort for most people. As discussed earlier, attachment-disordered children have typically experienced inconsistent accessibility to needs-provision, such that they become preoccupied with it. For these children the inability to consistently access needs-provision is a source of significant worry, further elevating their already chronically high levels of arousal. Chronically high levels of arousal make attachment-disordered children prone to problems of emotional and behavioural control (e.g. temper tantrums). In turn, problems of emotional and behavioural control bring attachment-disordered children into conflict with others, thereby reinforcing their perception of themselves as bad and others as uncaring (negative attachment representations). Negative attachment representations undermine trust in others and result in diminished expectations of deservedness in the attachment-disordered child. A lack of trust in others and low expectations of deservedness result in increased preoccupation with accessibility to needs-provision and worry about it, such that the cycle is perpetuated.

Although addressing one will create flow on effects in the others, the attachment-disordered child requires a response to each of the following: arousal, attachment representations and accessibility to needs provision. With regard to accessibility to needs provision, the attachment disordered child requires assistance to develop clear, consistent, successful and socially-approved strategies (e.g. asking where required, being self-reliant where appropriate) to access needs-provision. Hereafter, a number of methods to address accessibility preoccupations will be presented under the following headings:

- Verbalising understanding of accessibility preoccupations
- Emotional connectedness
- Emotional refuelling
- Sleep problems
- Organising need-seeking behaviour.

Verbalising understanding of accessibility preoccupations

In association with their excessive worry regarding adult accessibility and sensitive responsiveness, the attachment-disordered child is often preoccupied with maintaining engagement with, and control over, the behaviour and feelings of others. This manifests in excessive clinginess, attention-seeking behaviour, demanding behaviour, and overtly controlling and manipulative behaviours (e.g. superficial charm and/or bossiness). The purpose of these behaviours is to reassure the child regarding accessibility to needs-provision. Unfortunately, as many such behaviours are deemed age-inappropriate or otherwise deviant, and are either ignored or punished, the attachment-disordered child often experiences others as mean and uncaring, with resultant feelings of anger leading to distancing behaviour, followed by coercive attempts to re-connect. In order to address this, caregivers of attachment-disordered children should verbalise understanding of children's accessibility concerns, provide reassurance and explain to the child how to access needs-provision in a socially approved manner.

Statements that communicate understanding of accessibility preoccupations include the following:

- *I think that you believe that I will forget about you if we are not always together.*

- *I think that you believe I won't notice or understand when you really need me or something.*

- *You believe that if I don't do it now [get it for you] I will forget.*

- *You worry that I won't come back for you.*

- *You worry that I don't like you any more.*

- *You know you have done something wrong and you worry that I won't like or love you any more.*

Emotional connectedness

The attachment-disordered child's twin motivations to ensure accessibility and punish and distance caregivers creates conflicting behaviour that often leaves caregivers feeling like a yoyo. The attachment-disordered child draws the caregiver in to assure accessibility but, finding closeness uncomfortable, pushes them away again. A similar thing happens when an attachment-disordered child finds they cannot control caregiver behaviour to assure needs-provision. This kind of approach–avoid behaviour is synonymous with disorganised attachment representations that commonly result in an attachment disorder.

In order to avoid such cycling between closeness and distance, and reinforcing the same in the child, caregivers of attachment-disordered children are advised to maintain a smaller range of emotional connectedness to the child, being neither too close nor too distant. A consistent range of affect and associated behaviour such as this is reassuring for the attachment-disordered child, avoids over-stimulating them and puts the adult back in control of their own emotional presentation.

This approach can be extended to the caregiver's management of aberrant behaviour and affect. When the child is misbehaving, some accepted wisdom argues that it is best to ignore this. However, doing so simply increases the child's accessibility concerns, leading to an exacerbation of the problem. A better strategy is for the caregiver to show a degree of genuine emotion and verbalise the rest (e.g. *I can see you are angry. I am angry too* [slightly angry tone]. *Why don't we have a hug so we both feel better?*). It is important for the caregiver to show a degree of emotion as this represents an 'attunement experience', whereby the child feels emotionally connected to the adult, which is what they crave (and which typically manifests in their coercive attempts to make others feel bad because they do). By the caregiver using this strategy, the child feels understood and not threatened by too much closeness or distance, and this gives the caregiver the opportunity to intervene and soothe.

Emotional refuelling

By the age of approximately five months most infants become very selective about who they want to respond to their needs. Prior to this they are generally happy to be cared for by any caring adult. From five months of age they tend to want the adult or adults who care for them the most. This is when the attachment relationship is actively developing and emerging. Quality of parental care is particularly important during this period in influencing the type of attachment that will develop.

From about the age of eight months the infant develops the capacity to move about their environment. Once they can do so, secure infants will begin to explore their environment while also seeking temporary reunions with their preferred caregivers for 'emotional refuelling'. As a result of repeated experiences of separation, reunion and emotional refuelling, secure infants develop an appreciation of the fact that their caregivers are accessible, and that they can depend on their caring adults to be aware of and responsive to their needs without the requirement of being with them all of the time. In effect, they learn that they can devolve responsibility for needs-provision to the person or persons whom they experience as sensitive and responsive to their needs and better able to cope with their world (i.e. the attachment figures).

However, some attachment-disordered children, being drastically short on secure feelings, can display a tendency to seek an inordinate amount of emotional refuelling from their primary caregivers. As a result they are often perceived to be clingy and overdemanding of closeness to their caregivers. Most prefer to keep their caregivers close by and under their direct influence in order to be assured of needs-provision. However, as the people whom they first loved and depended upon were also the people who hurt them or let them down, the attachment-disordered child will also reject closeness to their current caregivers. The result is that attachment-disordered children alternate between a need for closeness to their current caregivers and a need to distance them. This is confusing and distressing to many caregivers of attachment-disordered children, who feel like they are on an emotional rollercoaster, from which they choose to exit by means of themselves seeking too much closeness to, or distance from, the child. The result is a strengthening of the attachment-disordered child's approach–avoid behaviour as they redouble their efforts to keep their caregivers under their direct influence, and at a safe emotional distance. Keeping their caregivers under their influence is especially important to attachment-disordered children as it engenders feelings of safety and well-being in association with a perception that they can control their accessibility to needs-provision.

What is called 'emotional refuelling in reverse' is a useful strategy that involves the caregiver of the attachment-disordered child checking in on the child at regular intervals prior to the child initiating closeness (and, subsequently, distance) – that is, the caregiver moves away from the child but frequently and regularly checks in on them. Checking in on the child might range from sharing a brief hug to simply letting the child know that you are nearby. Emotional refuelling in reverse can be extended to anticipating and responding to the child's needs prior to the child doing anything to elicit a caregiver response.

Emotional refuelling in reverse puts the caring adult back in control of the provision of secure feelings. This is very important because until such time as the attachment-disordered child is exposed to adult caregiving behaviour that occurs independently of any action on their part they will continue to believe that the *only* way to access needs-provision from adults is to be in charge themselves. This also assists the child to better tolerate the required degree of physical and emotional separation referred to above (see 'Emotional connectedness'). In addition, it reassures the attachment-disordered child that, though they may not be physically present, caring adults are aware of their child and concerned about their needs and well-being. In doing so, it represents a further step towards promoting secure attachment representations and reducing anxiety/arousal.

An example of where the use of emotional refuelling in reverse might be applied is with children who have difficulty with bedtime and achieving sleep onset.

Sleep problems

Sleep is a situation that involves increased separation, and increased separation is anxiety-evoking for many children, particularly insecure and attachment-disordered children. Anxiety involves heightened levels of arousal and heightened levels of arousal are not conducive to sleep onset. Many children protest at separation and will follow after their caregivers. Others will call out and/or leave their bedrooms in search of their caregivers. Others still will seek to sleep in the bed of their caregivers, or seek to have their caregiver sleep in the child's own bed.

Where the above sleep problems exist, emotional refuelling in reverse assists with keeping the child in their bed, promotes tolerance of separation and facilitates sleep onset by reducing arousal. Emotional refuelling in reverse for sleep involves the caregiver advising the child that they will return shortly to check in on them. The caregiver should define 'shortly' either through the use of time (e.g. five minutes) or some activity that has temporal relevance to the child (e.g. *I'll be back to check on you just as soon as I have put the kettle on/made a coffee*). The caregiver should ensure that they return at least two times before the child goes to sleep, so the child is reassured that the caregiver will return. The caregiver should advise the child that they should try to stay awake until the caregiver returns. This kind of 'paradoxical intention' (or 'reverse psychology' as it is more currently known) circumvents battles, which is important because battles regarding sleep onset will increase the child's arousal and are counter-productive to initiating sleep onset. Rather, content in the knowledge that they have permission to stay awake and that the caregiver will check in on them, the child will often fall asleep quickly and without fuss.

Organising need-seeking behaviour

A 'token system' represents a methodology for organising the child's attempts to secure needs-provision under conditions where the child's caregivers will be anticipating and responding to the child's usual daily needs. It involves providing the child with a finite number of tokens each day and explaining to the child that each time they want the caring adult to attend and respond to a reasonable perceived need they need to hand the adult a token, where a reasonable perceived need would include the need for a snack, drink or the caregiver's involvement in an activity of the child's choosing and an unreasonable perceived need would include demands for inappropriate foods or new toys, or the monopolisation of the caregiver's time. The amount of tokens given to a child depends on their age and neediness and the accessibility and likely responsiveness of the caring adult. Ten tokens may be sufficient for some children for the span of one full day with a caring adult. A smaller number may be sufficient for school-aged children during the school week. If the child is able, they should be encouraged to verbalise their perceived need. If not, or if the adult can accurately do so, the adult should verbalise what they think the child's perceived need is. The caring adult should make certain that the child is only given sufficient tokens to ensure that the caring adult can respond to all reasonable requests presented in this way, either straight away or soon after the token is presented (the use of *yes, when...* can be useful in regard to the latter – see later). It is permissible to respond to other needs that the child has without the presentation of the token, where it is the adult who anticipates and initiates needs-provision (e.g. the need for three main meals per day and the need to go to sleep in the evening).

When the tokens run out, the caring adult should continue to respond to basic needs (e.g. food, warmth, protection) and reassure the child regarding this. The caring adult should remind the child to use their tokens wisely before they use them all in a given day. In the face of persistent demands, the caring adult may say to the child something like: *That is something I would do anyway; do you really want to use a token for that?* After the first week, the number of tokens can be reduced slightly, and again after each week thereafter. After not less than two weeks, perceived needs expressed in a socially sanctioned manner can be responded to once all the child's tokens have been exhausted. That is, the caregiver should continue to respond to the child's requests for a response to a reasonable perceived need after their daily allocation of tokens has been exhausted in order to reinforce appropriate needs expression. However, if the child becomes overwhelmingly demanding again, the caring adult should consider re-instituting the token system from the beginning.

In the writer's experience, attachment-disordered children attempt to ensure that their tokens last an entire day, thus providing the caring adult with welcome relief from constant demands. Attachment-disordered children become less demanding because the presence of tokens is reassuring to them. They have a system by which they can consistently and successfully access needs-provision. In addition, the system encourages the development and use of socially sanctioned perceived need expression. To the extent that the system engenders consistent sensitive responsiveness from caring adults,

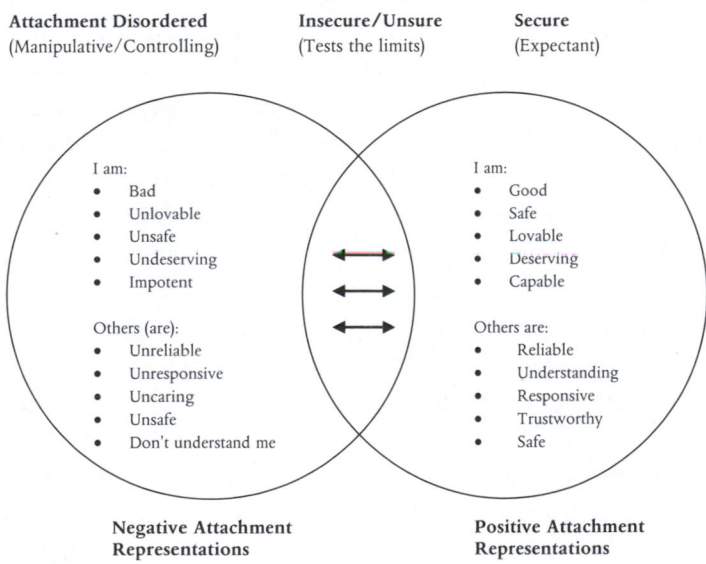

Figure 3.2 Attachment security and representations regarding self and other

reduces anti-social behaviour and reassures the child, the twin goals of reducing arousal and promoting positive attachment representations are promoted.

CHANGES IN ATTACHMENT REPRESENTATIONS

The attachment representations under which children operate fluctuate to an extent, as illustrated by the use of arrows in Figure 3.2. Classifications of 'secure', 'insecure' and 'attachment disordered' are meant to reflect the attachment representations under which the child operates *predominantly*. All people have times when they feel insecure or that the world is against them. Attachment-disordered children can experience periods of relative security. Caregivers of attachment-disordered children report that they can often tell which attachment representations predominate by the facial expressions and tone of voice exhibited by the child when they get up in the morning. They commonly misattribute this to 'split personality' or multiple personalities, which arises in cases of extreme trauma and fragmented identity development. Because attachment representations are fluid and malleable, even the most disturbed children can be helped to hold, and operate increasingly in accordance with, positive attachment representations.

Attachment representations can be influenced by both external factors (e.g. parenting, psychotherapy) and internal ones (e.g. sleep/dreams, thoughts/cognitions). Insecure and attachment-disordered children can thereby be encouraged to accept new and more helpful perceptions of themselves, others and their place in the world in association with attention to specific aspects of parental care. Psychotherapy can also be influential in fostering adherence to positive attachment representations, particularly in terms of challenging negative attachment representations and associated unhelpful cognitions (thoughts).

Hereafter, a number of methods to change attachment representations will be presented under the following headings:

- Be all-powerful, all-understanding, all-knowing
- Hold appropriate developmental expectations
- Respond to the need as well as the behaviour
- Verbalise the child's thoughts and feelings
- When the request is reasonable but the timing is poor
- Engage in interactive repair.

Be all-powerful, all-understanding, all-knowing

An attachment figure is a person the child goes to when they are sick, sad, hurt, scared. They are a person whom the child perceives to be better able to cope with circumstances that are painful, stressful, or frightening. They are a source of comfort and protection for the child. In order to be an attachment figure and to be a source of comfort, support and protection for the child, a caregiver needs to be seen by the child as being more powerful, more knowing and more understanding than the child. From the child's perspective, such a strong person can protect the child in all circumstances. If a child is allowed to be the boss they will never feel truly secure. Similarly, if a child has no boundaries or expectations placed upon them by an authoritative adult, they will think that adults do not care.

One approach that casts the adult in an all-knowing role and facilitates the child's acceptance of adult authority is teaching the child a new game or activity. Introducing a controlling and otherwise difficult child to a fun or interesting new activity and teaching them how to do it often creates a unique situation where the attachment-disordered child will accept adult authority and direction in association with being motivated to learn a desired activity or game (e.g. chess). In addition, if the activity is fun, the child experiences pleasure in association with learning and accepting direction from a caring adult. With repeated exposure to such experiences, the child instinctively experiences pleasure and other desirable feelings in association with adults being in charge and teaching them. Psychologists refer to this process as 'classical conditioning' and the response engendered by a particular stimulus as a 'conditioned response'. It is possible that the desirable conditioned response will generalise to other aspects of the child's life where they experience the adult in an authoritative role.

Play is also important in the re-mediation (amelioration) of attachment disorders for other reasons. Play:

- offers opportunity for attunement experiences

- promotes positive conceptions of self and other, and

- allows the adult to structure and organise the behaviour and affective displays of the child in a non-threatening manner.

Where a child is likely to be contrary, and where you want to direct them regarding your wishes and their compliance is non-negotiable, do not ask the child, *tell* the child. If you *ask* them, you are effectively giving them a choice regarding whether to comply or not. If they say 'no', you are then in a lose–lose situation, in that they either do not do what you expect of them or you precipitate a confrontation that can have the effect of upsetting and alienating the child.

Children respond better to directions and outcomes rather than directions and punishments e.g., *Pick up your toys and you can go out and play*, rather than *Pick up your toys or you're grounded*. Nevertheless, where children remain defiant and discipline is warranted, express empathy for the child's feelings, but follow through with directions and consequences. Don't allow the child to set an emotional tone of anger and hostility.

As a result of their experience of unreliable and unresponsive parenting, attachment-disordered children have learned that the only person they can rely on is themselves. This often manifests as an intense need to control their environment and everything in it, including the thoughts, feelings and behaviours of others, a goal they achieve through naughty, coercive/manipulative behaviour. A power struggle can therefore often ensue when the child's caregivers attempt to assert normal adult authority and direct the child. Attachment-disordered children often enjoy engaging in power struggles and experience a compulsion to win them. Borrowing from principles implicit in martial arts, the 'push–pull' approach uses the child's intense desire for control to reinforce adult authority. This is achieved when, rather than directing a child regarding inconsequential (to the adult) matters (e.g. which breakfast cereal to eat, which shirt to wear, which television programme to watch during TV time) an adult caregiver offers the child choices and reinforces that they can make this decision. This strategy meets the child's need for control while also reinforcing the adult's authority through the offering of choices.

Finally, paradoxical intention (as mentioned earlier when looking at the issue of sleep) is a particularly effective short-term strategy for circumventing the attachment-disordered child's attempts to regulate the emotional closeness of caring adults through affective displays – thus facilitating adult control over this important aspect of the relationship with the attachment-disordered child. For instance, some attachment-disordered children have a tendency to frown and project an outward attitude of hostility or anger in an attempt to distance caring adults. Under such circumstances, the author verbalises to the child that they are right to frown and/or look serious, sad or angry as this is a serious, sad or frustrating time. Furthermore, they are right to not smile. Invariably the child starts to smile. The caring adult should playfully remind them that this is a serious, sad or frustrating time and smiling is not appropriate. The child will then seek to stop smiling, only to burst into laughter. The caring adult should state that it is certainly not a time for laughter. By this time the serious, sad or angry child is in an emotional state fit for meaningful engagement.

Hold appropriate developmental expectations

The fundamental goal of parenting attachment-disordered children should be to assist them to increasingly adopt and live by more secure attachment representations of themselves and others. In achieving this goal, it is important to view the behaviour of attachment-disordered children as *developmentally appropriate,* if not *age-appropriate.* Development unfolds in a sequence of steps built on previous successes and achievements, and these children have experienced inconsistent needs-provision, major disruptions and losses that have been disruptive of their social and emotional development. In effect, they have social and emotional needs that are akin to those of a very young child. Their attempts to get their needs met are reflected in behavioural strategies and affective displays that are also typically used by *very young children* to draw attention to their needs and to derive feelings of safety and security. These children generally:

- do not verbalise their needs
- fail to regulate their negative affect, and
- engage in naughty behaviour and affective displays to draw attention to their needs, secure a caregiver response and ventilate pent-up anxiety/over-arousal.

Like other children, they require caregiver involvement and love, nurturance, guidance, acknowledgement and acceptance of a range of affect and soothing when they are distressed. However, unlike what is the case for other children, these children's caregivers may fail to respond to these needs because they become preoccupied with managing what they perceive to be the age-inappropriate, aberrant behaviour and affective displays that are the attachment-disordered child's main strategy for expressing their needs and feelings.

In contrast to the normal adult response when a baby cries loudly because he is hungry, it is a common occurrence by the time a child reaches school age for adults to expect children to express their needs (e.g. hunger) verbally and to admonish the child for behaviours that are considered to be inappropriate to context (e.g. crying for food), even if they are the child's way of expressing a need, in order to facilitate their learning regarding acceptable behaviour and needs expression, and conformity to societal expectations regarding these (Figure 3.3). This is a problem for attachment-disordered children, who express their needs primarily through behaviour. Attachment-disordered children require a *response to the need as well as the behaviour* that serves to draw attention to the need, in the same way that one responds to the behavioural expressions of a pre-verbal child (Figure 3.4). Without this, the child will

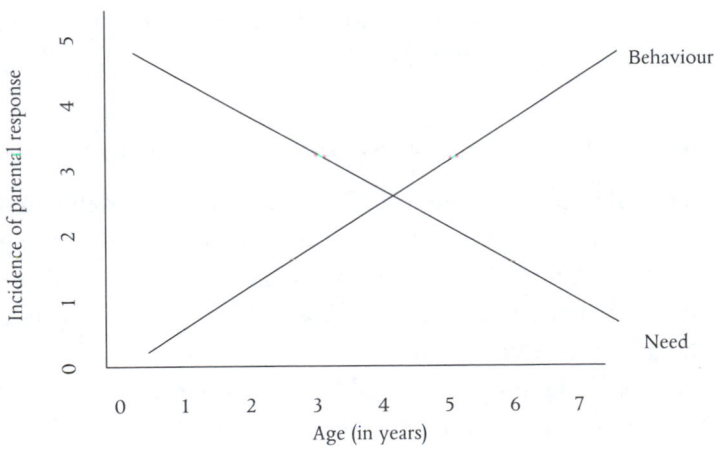

Figure 3.3 Normal patterns of caregiver response to behavioural expressions of needs in children

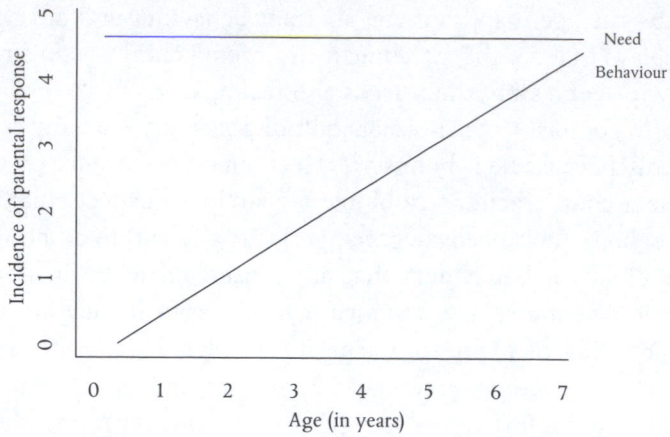

Figure 3.4 Required patterns of caregiver response to behaviour and needs in insecure and attachment-disordered children

continue to be unsure about the sensitivity and responsiveness of others to their needs, their perception of the reliability and trustworthiness of others will remain disturbed, and their capacity to empathise with others will be limited. The consequences of these include ongoing unregulated behaviour and affect, antisocial behaviour and a lifetime of impairment in their well-being and adjustment.

Respond to the need as well as the behaviour

Nearly all human behaviour is functional and purposeful, and children rarely misbehave for misbehaviour's sake. Among other things, misbehaviour can serve as an emotional release (such as when children are tired and over-aroused) or as a strategy to draw attention to an unmet need. Attachment-disordered and pre-verbal children are typically unable or unwilling to express their needs directly/verbally and do so through coercive behaviours.

From their first day, infants draw attention to their needs through affective displays that might later come to be viewed as developmentally inappropriate and anti-social. Babies learn that crying and screaming is an effective way to draw parental attention. It is not surprising that this broadens to other aberrant behaviour among toddlers, such as throwing objects, banging doors, turning the TV and lights off and on, etc. Such naughty behaviour typically attracts more attention than good behaviour. When the attachment-disordered child is misbehaving it is important to try to work out what unexpressed need might be giving rise to the behaviour rather than simply responding to the behaviour.

Verbalise the child's thoughts and feelings

Attachment-disordered children typically communicate their thoughts and feelings through aberrant behaviours and affective displays. To encourage the child to use words, caregivers need to verbalise what they think the child is thinking about or feeling. Verbalising their thoughts and feelings often results in the child feeling heard and understood, is soothing to the child and makes them less likely to continue to use aberrant behaviour and affective displays to communicate their needs and wishes. This is a much more effective strategy than *asking* children how they feel or what they think because asking is akin to an admission to the child that you do not understand.

Examples of verbalising understanding include:

- *I can see you are cross. I think you believe that I am being mean/don't care/don't understand.*

- *You look happy. I think you had a good day today.*

- *They must have done something to make you mad. I guess they did something that was unfair/mean/nasty.*

- *I can see you feel bad because you know you did something wrong and think I will not like you any more.*

When the request is reasonable but the timing is poor

Conventional wisdom suggests that children need to accommodate to the refusal of some of their requests. That is, they need sometimes to hear 'no'. Nevertheless, they also need to hear 'yes' and have their requests responded to and validated. Demanding children will make many requests of their caregivers and become increasingly demanding, unsettled and alienated when they experience frequent rejection of their wishes. Attachment-disordered children also often experience exaggerated feelings of rejection in association with hearing 'no'. Both groups of children may defiantly do what they please in anticipation of a negative parental response, which then results in loss of parental authority and disruption to caregiver–child relationships. Saying *'yes, when...'* avoids a confrontation, reinforces caregiver authority and promotes a more positive perception of caregiver understanding and responsiveness. It is also a useful strategy for getting children to perform required chores (e.g. *yes, you can go next door to play when you have dried the dishes*). Furthermore, it avoids a perception of parental inconsistency, and reinforcing persistent demanding behaviour, which can arise in the context of caring adults initially saying 'no' and later saying 'yes' in response to persistent demanding.

Engage in interactive repair

Attachment-disordered children often experience a deep sense of shame in association with caregiver admonishments. Unaddressed, this shame can promote ill-feeling towards the caregiver and further distance the child, which, ultimately, is counter-productive in terms of achieving a close and loving caregiver–child relationship. After intervening in relation to a child's behaviour it is important to remind them that you still love them or make some other statements reflecting their positive attributes.

MANAGING AROUSAL

As mentioned earlier, attachment-disturbed children are chronically over-aroused, with the result that they engage in aberrant behaviours and affective displays in order to release anxiety and restore feelings of well-being. A critical aspect of caring for these children, therefore, is managing their arousal levels. Previously discussed strategies to address accessibility preoccupations and change attachment representations are also helpful in alleviating anxiety and reducing arousal levels. For example, communicating sensitivity and understanding of their thoughts, feelings and accessibility concerns/preoccupations through the use of verbalisation and empathy is soothing to these children.

Other strategies that are useful in addressing arousal problems include playing quiet classical music while the child sleeps. The rationale here is that the brain is still attending to stimuli in the child's environment while they are sleeping. Intervening to ensure that these stimuli are soothing is helpful in reducing the child's arousal levels. Caregivers of children who utilise this method report that the child sleeps more soundly and wakes in a happier mood. Relaxation and meditation are also likely to be useful, as are opportunities to engage in physical activity. Carefully managing the child's exposure to settings and situations where there is a lot of external stimulation (e.g. shopping centres), including many things they cannot control, is generally warranted.

PUTTING IT ALL TOGETHER

While the behaviour of children with attachment difficulties is probably of the most immediate concern, it is important that the primary focus is on developing positive relationships, because without this context, no behaviour-management strategies will be effective. Children with attachment difficulties are likely to interpret discipline as arbitrary and cruel, so directions and consequences (i.e. punishment) need to be delivered calmly and with empathy rather than with anger. In order to help the child deal with their feelings of shame and rage, interactive repair should be provided as soon as possible after discipline so that the child knows that they will not be rejected because of their behaviour.

Figure 3.5 illustrates how the above parenting suggestions can be incorporated into day-to-day behaviour management.

- In the first step, the child engages in some form of misbehaviour. Rather than verbally admonishing the child or instituting some form of punishment (e.g. time-out), it is important first to take stock of the circumstances under which the behaviour occurred and to verbalise

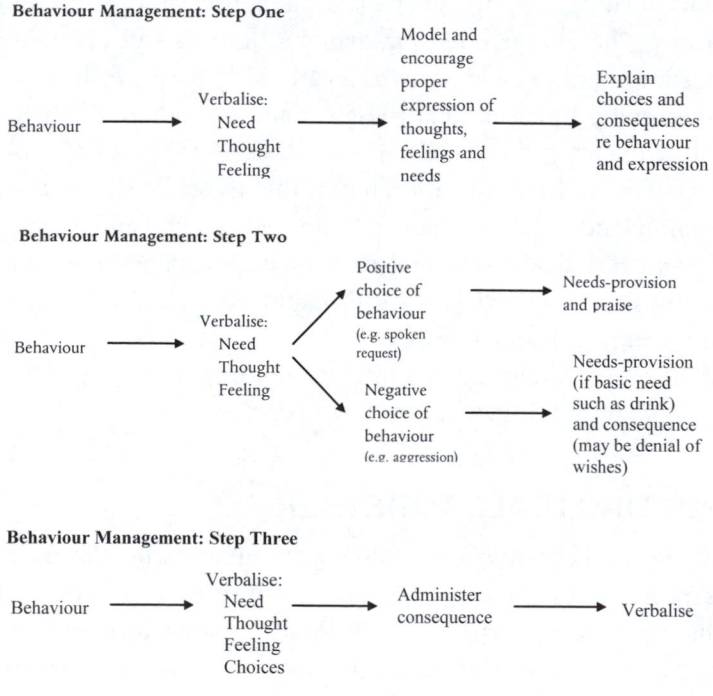

Figure 3.5 Behaviour management: Putting the pieces together

understanding regarding the need, the thought and/ or the feeling that gave rise to the behaviour.

- Next, a caregiver should model for the child, and encourage, proper expression of thoughts, feelings and needs. Then, the caregiver should explain to the child that they have choices regarding their expression of the aforementioned, and the different consequences (or outcomes) that arise from each choice.

- Only after these two steps are followed should the caregiver discipline the child.

When the author's youngest child was three years of age (i.e. newly/incompletely verbal) he would, at times, call out 'hungry' or 'thirsty'. At other times he had a habit of standing at the refrigerator, looking to see if anyone had noticed him, stomping his foot and affecting a grumpy facial expression. If no one responded to his signal that he was hungry or thirsty or both he would angrily stomp his foot and pull off various notices held to the refrigerator with magnets and throw them to the floor. At such times the author might have chosen to verbally admonish the child and require him to put the notices back on the refrigerator door. However, to do so would have further upset him as he would have interpreted the author's response as lacking understanding and being uncaring.

Instead, I would say the following: '*H, I see that you are standing at the fridge and that you are cross. I understand that you think that no one has noticed that you would like a drink.*'

H would sullenly acknowledge '*Yes*'.

I would then say: '*Well, H, you need to say "Please Daddy, may I have a drink."*'

He would quietly and sullenly say '*Please, Daddy, may I have something to drink?*'

I would then say '*A bit louder and nicely.*'

He would say, more loudly and in more polite tones, '*Please, Daddy, may I have something to drink?*'

I would respond with '*Of course, you can. I will get it for you straight away. I will always get you a drink when you need it. All you have to do is say "Please, Daddy, may I have something to drink?" However, if you don't ask and stand at the fridge and stomp, I may get you a drink but I will also tell you off for making a mess of the notices on the fridge. I will even ask you to put them all back.*'

Although H was only three years of age, this is a vivid example of step one and can be easily applied to the older, attachment-disordered child. Thankfully, the author did not have to proceed to step two and three with H.

In the second step, the child subsequently engages in some form of behaviour, good or bad, associated with the aforementioned thought, feeling or need. On this occasion the caregiver again verbalises understanding of the thought, feeling or need. In the event that the child drew attention to the thought, feeling or need using pro-social behaviour, the caregiver responds with praise and needs-provision. In the event that the child drew attention to the thought, feeling or need using anti-social behaviour, the child is admonished and a consequence may be instituted. Nevertheless, the need is acknowledged and an outcome is negotiated for needs-provision. A caregiver should always respond to the need as well as the behaviour (for example, '*I can see that you are angry and that you think no one has noticed that you would like a drink. We have already spoken about how you should use your words when you would like a drink. I will give you a drink but I would like you to sit in your room for a few moments while I get it.*')

The final step relates to when a child has made a poor choice regarding the expression of a thought, feeling or need, and a consequence is instituted. The child may become angry and/or distressed regarding the imposition of a consequence. They need to know that there is a rationale as to *why* a consequence is instituted and that the caregiver understands their thoughts and feeling regarding the consequence. If this important step is missed the attachment-disordered child is likely to form their own pessimistic, maladaptive view regarding the intentions of the adult – hence, the caregiver verbalises understanding and reminds the child that they have the child's best interests in mind when instituting consequences for undesirable behaviours (*'I can see that you are angry that I am sending you to your room and think I am being mean. However, as your parent it is my job to love and care for you and to help you make good choices about behaviour. When I punish you it is to help you to remember to make good choices in future.'*)

ADDITIONAL CONSIDERATIONS

The care requirements of attachment-disordered children are significant, yet parental care alone may not be sufficient to promote the development of, and adherence to, secure attachment representations in these chldren. Attachment-disordered children will require intervention at the environmental (home and school) and individual levels. Psychotherapy is an important component of the re-mediation of their attachment problems. Caregivers and teachers of attachment-disordered children also benefit from psycho-education from practitioners specialised in providing advice regarding the care of these children and so, often, the involvement of a knowledgeable psychotherapist is a requirement in such cases.

MATTHEW'S STORY (CONTINUED)

During the initial consultation with Matthew's foster parent, Helen, she reported that she had read numerous books on traumatised and attachment-disordered children and obtained information off the Internet, but that nothing she did to manage Matthew's behaviour seemed to work consistently. In fact, she described a pattern whereby she would try something new, it would work for a while, then it would start to lose its effectiveness, and she would be forced to try a new strategy or approach. One intervention approach that consistently did not work was behaviour management. In particular, sending Matthew to his room for 'time-out' precipitated a dramatic deterioration in his emotional state and behaviour. Withdrawal of prized items and privileges from Matthew only appeared to increase his resentment, notwithstanding the fact that he would state 'don't care' as the last of his toys were being taken from his room. She concluded that love was not enough for a child like Matthew, and that he was not particularly lovable anyway.

In response to the above, the psychotherapist advised Helen that maintaining a consistent approach to his care and management was important. As tactfully as could be achieved, he explained that repeated changes in management approach created an inconsistent care environment that was itself unsettling for Matthew. He advocated the implementation and maintenance of a small number of strategies known to address accessibility preoccupations, negative beliefs about self and other, and over-arousal/anxiety. He reassured Helen that these approaches were part of the normal range of parenting behaviour, and hence represented fine-tuning of parenting rather than a radically different approach. He acknowledged that Matthew's behaviour might get worse before it got better as he coercively attempted to reinstitute Helen's usual pattern of relating to him. He explained that Matthew's behaviour in this regard represented his own attempts to reassure himself that his beliefs about how his world worked were still valid. He advised that an important component of parenting approaches that would be recommended was that they would increase Helen's power in the relationship with Matthew. He explained that only through being an all-powerful, all-understanding, all-knowing caregiver who could fix all challenges that Matthew faced in day-to-day life would Matthew relinquish his controlling and self-reliant behaviour and depend increasingly on her, such that he felt safe in his world, valued relationships and attempted to conform to conventional standards of behaviour. He also advised that Matthew would benefit from teaching staff at his school implementing a similar care and management approach and advised how it is his usual practice to approach the school and offer to provide general training to all school staff regarding key aspects of the care and management of an attachment-disordered child, with follow-up interactions with key personnel regarding more specific strategies.

With regard to Helen's own feelings of revulsion towards Matthew, as expressed in her perception of him being unlovable, the psychotherapist reassured her that this was a common occurrence for caregivers of attachment-disordered children. The psychotherapist also reassured her that love of a child grows in association with shared positive experiences and the feeling of being important to the child. The psychotherapist further reassured Helen that the possibility of shared positive experiences and of feeling important to the child, like love, would grow in association with Matthew experiencing her as understanding, accessible and responsive, and she herself having the perception and experience of being a capable parent and positive influence in his life.

The psychotherapist provided Helen with a comprehensive written guide to understanding attachment and attachment disorder, as well as the care and management requirements of attachment-disordered children. He also supplied her with a CD containing orchestral lullabies. He encouraged her to play the music quietly in Matthew's room when he went to bed and throughout the entire night. He explained that the purpose of this intervention was to lower Matthew's cortical (brain) arousal levels in a manner that required little effort on the part of the child and his foster parent. He further explained that the intervention was anticipated to work because the brain still attends to external stimuli while the child is asleep and a benefit would be achieved by these stimuli being soothing.

In addition, the psychotherapist coached Helen in how to

verbalise her understanding of Matthew's thoughts, feelings, intentions and accessibility preoccupations. He advised that the use of verbalisation of understanding increased engagement with the child, reassured the child that they were understood and cared about, facilitated the development of a belief in adult omnipotence in the child, and modelled the use of language to express aspects of his internal world as opposed to using behaviour as a primary mode of expression. The psychotherapist advised that verbalising understanding was the cornerstone of any caregiver intervention with attachment-disordered children as it could be used to address accessibility preoccupations, promoted a positive sense of self and other, and was reassuring to the child, such that it lowered arousal/anxiety. However, the psychotherapist warned Helen not to overdo it by including verbalisation of Matthew's positive feelings, as achieving too much emotional closeness too quickly (particularly in relation to painful emotions) might result in Matthew engaging in distancing behaviour. He advised that where this occurred Helen should verbalise understanding that Matthew was not always comfortable with people knowing what he was thinking or feeling.

Finally, the psychotherapist advised Helen to check in on Matthew whenever he was doing something independently, anticipate his needs before his engaging in any behaviour to secure needs-provision, and surprise him with so-called 'random acts of kindness' (e.g. providing his favourite snack or milkshake without any warning or explanantion). He explained that such parenting behaviour represented a subtle way of introducing Matthew to the experience of people caring, understanding and responding to his needs and wishes without him having to do something to make it so – that is, it became a way of introducing Matthew to the idea that he did not always have to control others in order to get his needs met (which is something that it would have been difficult for him to learn on his own given the extent of his controlling behaviours). In addition, this intervention represented a way of promoting more positive representations regarding the attitudes and intentions of others and his own deservedness of positive interpersonal experiences.

Over the ensuing weeks the psychotherapist met regularly with Helen, either before or after one of Matthew's scheduled sessions, or separately from them. During these meetings the psychotherapist engaged in further fine-tuning of the above interventions, particularly the use of verbalisation of understanding. In addition, after achieving a meaningful rapport with Matthew the psychotherapist incorporated Helen in sessions in order to facilitate positive engagement between them, such as through modelling and encouraging verbalisation of understanding and engagement in mutually enjoyable play activities. Over a period of a few weeks, Helen reported that Mathew was calmer, less demanding and more inclined to express his reasonable needs verbally. However, approximately three months after the intervention commenced she reported that Matthew was becoming unsettled and unreasonably demanding and controlling again, such that she was again feeling dispirited and defeated. The psychotherapist reassured her that such setbacks were expected. He explained that, as she became emotionally closer to Matthew and he valued their relationship, Matthew would experience stronger feelings of shame associated with minor misdemeanours and seek to withdraw from engagement with, and dependency on, others as a defence against experiencing this powerful aversive emotion. The psychotherapist advised Helen that, more than ever, Matthew needed to be reassured that she would go on caring for him no matter what misbehaviour he engaged in and she needed to maintain the parenting interventions the psychotherapist had suggested and continue to provide verbal understanding and reassurance regarding his shame.

CHAPTER SUMMARY

- Secure attachments benefit both the child and the broader community.

- The care requirements of attachment-disordered children are akin to those of very young children.

- Adults need to be 'all-powerful', 'all-understanding' and 'all-caring' in the eyes of the attachment-disordered child.

- All behaviour exhibited by the attachment-disordered child is purposeful and requires a response to the *reason* that gave rise to the behaviour *as well as* the behaviour itself.

- Reassuring attachment-disordered children about accessibility to needs-provision, promoting optimism regarding self and other, and managing arousal are essential and interrelated components of the care of the attachment-disordered child.

CHAPTER 4

TREATING THE ATTACHMENT-DISORDERED CHILD – WHAT TO EXPECT

WHAT CONSTITUTES EFFECTIVE TREATMENT?

Effective treatment of attachment-disordered children necessarily involves education of caregivers and professionals who work with the child (e.g. teachers, social workers) regarding the care and management requirements of these children and the implementation of relational and caring behaviour that promotes the development of, and adherence to, secure attachment representations, as discussed in the previous chapter. In addition, the effective treatment of attachment-disordered children incorporates the provision of psychotherapy. 'Psychotherapy' can be defined here as a methodology by which psychological theories and methods are used in the treatment of mental disorders. In the case of attachment disorder, the most relevant psychological theory is Attachment Theory. Nevertheless, as has been presented in this book, other psychological theories of development and learning are also important. Effective psychological methods include play therapies, attachment-oriented psychotherapies and cognitive–behavioural therapies.

- Play therapies involve the use of games and other play activities that secure the child's engagement, facilitate emotional expression and social learning, and promote a positive perception of self, other and relatedness to others. Through repeated experience of affective attunement that arises in the context of play, the child experiences (perhaps for the first time) an emotional union with the therapist that promotes a perception that they are understood, that their emotions are valid and that they are cherished. Play therapies are particularly useful in the early stages of psychotherapy, with young children and with resistant children.

- Attachment-oriented psychotherapies involve the psychotherapist in developing a relationship with the child whereby the psychotherapist takes on a kind of parental role. The psychotherapist interacts with the child in a way that facilitates safe expression of fears, anxieties and unhelpful beliefs regarding self, other and the world. The psychotherapist conveys unconditional understanding and acceptance of the child, despite the child's likely attempts to achieve their own rejection by the therapist. By relating to the child in a sensitive, understanding and authoritative manner and modelling appropriate relational behaviour, the psychotherapist seeks to establish a new template, or model, for relatedness to others (with associated adaptive, that is helpful, beliefs about self, other and world) that might be expected to generalise to other key relationships.

- Cognitive–behavioural therapies incorporate the use of activities and dialogue targeted at identifying (verbalising) and challenging unhelpful beliefs about self, other and the world (attachment representations) and promoting adherence to an alternative, functional belief system. The child may, for example, be set tasks to accomplish that facilitate positive social learning and promote the development and maintenance of secure-attachment representations. Tasks take the form of behavioural experiments, such as the child telling a teacher that they do not understand a piece of work they have been given to do, and reporting on how the teacher responded. Because of their reliance on verbal interaction, cognitive–behavioural therapies are more applicable to children of seven to eight years and older.

A STRENGTHS PERSPECTIVE

In addition, caregivers of attachment-disordered children should expect the psychotherapist to operate from what is called a 'strengths perspective' – that is, their focus will be on promoting attributions, knowledge and skills that strengthen the child, as opposed to weakening the child in any way. Hence, the psychotherapist will carefully avoid reinforcing unhelpful deficit attributions and beliefs, such as victim and perpetrator orientations. Instead, a skilled psychotherapist will focus on identifying and re-mediating the circumstances that gave rise to aberrant and maladaptive behaviour and affective displays.

To illustrate, we can take the example of children who engage in sexualised behaviour with other children. Too often, upon the behaviour coming to light, people try to classify the actions of the child in terms of them being a victim or perpe-trator of sexual abuse. But too little consideration is given to the impact of both formulations.

- On the one hand, the identified victim is likely to take

on unhelpful attributions about themselves as dirty, damaged goods whose life is ruined (either through the misguided solicitations of caring adults or their own awareness of how society perceives sexual-abuse victims). In addition, the identified victim may form a belief that others cannot be trusted and that they are therefore unsafe and at risk of further exploitation. Paradoxically, the anxiety arising from such self-attributions can result in overly inhibited or disinhibited relational behaviour, each of which has the potential to impact adversely on the child's adjustment.

- On the other hand, through sanctions placed upon them and attempts to remediate their 'deviant' behaviour, the identified perpetrator is encouraged to adopt a perception of themselves as having done something disgusting, and of therefore being deviant and a risk to others. This invariably leads to feelings of alienation from others and a breakdown in stable and supportive social networks. The end result is reduced access to mainstream social networks for needs-provision and a greater likelihood of further aberrant behaviour.

CAREGIVER PARTICIPATION IN PSYCHOTHERAPY

In order for the treatment of attachment-disordered children to be truly effective, caregivers need to be involved in the intervention process. Caregiver involvement might include direct participation in psychotherapy sessions such as occurs in some Play Therapy approaches (e.g. Theraplay[25]). More typically, caregiver involvement takes the form of being recipients of psychoeducation, support and guidance regarding the care and management of their attachment-disordered child. Where caregivers are separated, it can be important for both parties to be involved in the psychotherapy process, though the participation of the primary caregiver is the minimum requirement and the parties would usually attend separate sessions. This latter scenario is important where the former couple share an acrimonious relationship and/or when attending jointly might facilitate in the child an unrealistic hope of a family reconciliation. In addition, as major caregivers for children, classroom teachers might also be incorporated into the psychotherapy process by being in receipt of psycho-education closely aligned to that received by the parent(s).

SOME SECRETS ABOUT HOW ATTACHMENT-DISORDERED CHILDREN CAN BE ENGAGED IN PSYCHOTHERAPY

Psychotherapy participants can be divided into two groups, voluntary and involuntary.

- Voluntary participants typically initiate their own referral to a psychotherapist and are motivated to participate in the treatment process. Their prospects for the re-mediation of the issue that precipitated them seeking psychotherapy are good, especially where a strong therapeutic alliance is achieved between participant and therapist.

- Involuntary participants are typically asked or required to attend psychotherapy by a third party or agency. Their motivation to participate in psychotherapy is therefore variable. Similarly, the prospects of them achieving re-mediation of the issue that precipitated their referral to a psychotherapist is also variable.

It is therefore likely that treatment outcomes will be better for a participant who is a voluntary participant in psychotherapy, than for an involuntary participant.

Attachment-disordered children will almost certainly be involuntary participants, to begin with. Invariably, they will not have chosen to attend psychotherapy and this decision will usually have been made by a caring adult. They are also likely to perceive that psychotherapy has been organised in response to something that they have done; that is, in response to something they have done that is *bad*. They are likely to think, by extension, that *they* are bad, and that the caring adult who brings them to psychotherapy also thinks so. In addition, they may believe that the psychotherapist is a stranger who *knows about* their badness and will do something, the child knows not what, to them because of their badness – all of which increase the child's anxiety and reluctance to engage and participate in psychotherapy. Because attachment-disordered children perceive that their actions are justified and that adults either do not understand or do not care, they will almost certainly perceive the requirement to attend psychotherapy as being unfair. In instances where the attachment-disordered child has siblings who live with them, the referred child may interpret their own referral for psychotherapy as further evidence that their caregivers do not love them as much as their brothers/sisters. As attachment-disordered children already have a poor self-concept and are susceptible to maladaptive behaviour and emotional displays in association with this, a focus on their problematic behaviour gives rise to feelings of shame, making it even less likely that the child will want to attend psychotherapy and increasing the likelihood of further aberrant behaviour – all of which is hardly a promising starting point for psychotherapy.

In order to ensure that attachment-disordered children become willing participants in psychotherapy, caregivers need to verbalise understanding of the fears that such a referral is likely to precipitate in the child, and provide reassurance that they are instigating psychotherapy out of concern for the child's happiness. Attachment-disordered children might also be reassured about attending psychotherapy by telling them that it is actually likely to be *fun*. The child will benefit from being told that the psychotherapist is likely to be a lively and entertaining person who will play games and engage in other fun activities with them. Children are more likely to want to attend psychotherapy if they anticipate that aspects of it will be fun – and, to the extent that it *is* fun, this will reassure the child that the caregiver's concern is for the child's happiness.

In addition, another method a psychotherapist is likely to use to maintain the attachment-disordered child's engagement in the psychotherapy process is to relate to children at their own level and in relation to their interests. This is particularly useful amongst teenage participants. Attachment-disordered teenagers often adopt interests that fall outside of the mainstream for their age cohort as an expression of their feelings of difference and disconnectedness, such as immersing themselves in sub-cultures (e.g. gothic) or listening to alternative music (e.g. girls listening to heavy metal music). By taking an active interest in their interests the therapist not only builds rapport but nor-malises the child's non-mainstream interests, so that they ex-perience greater social integration and are then more likely to conform to conventional standards of behaviour, including the requirement that they attend and participate in psychotherapy. Greater conformity to conventional standards of behaviour is always achieved by improving social integration; that is, by developing a meaningful relationship between a child and caring adult. Attachment-disordered children are more likely to attend psychotherapy if they experience the adult as having a genuine interest in their own interests. Hence, caregivers of attachment-disordered children should expect that this will be an important aspect of psychotherapy.

Furthermore, caregivers of attachment-disordered children should expect that the psychotherapist will verbalise under-standing of the presenting problem *from the child's perspective*. Psychotherapists who are experienced in treating attachment-disordered children are knowledgeable about the way in which these children perceive themselves, others and their place in the world and the potential motivations behind their perceived problematical behaviour and affective displays, and will make educated guesses regarding these. In so doing, they will enable the child to feel fully heard, perhaps for the first time. Attachment-disordered children typically respond very well to this approach, though some severely attachment-disordered children find the degree of emotional connectedness achieved through verbalisation too confronting in the early stages of psychotherapy, with the result that they push the therapist away. Under such circumstances, the caregiver should continue to encourage the child to attend psychotherapy as fear of emotional closeness will never be overcome through avoidance of it.

MATTHEW'S STORY (CONTINUED)

When Matthew arrived for his first psychotherapy session he was reluctant to engage in therapeutic conversations and was more intent on testing the limits of what he could get away with in the unfamiliar setting of the psychotherapist's office. His reluctance to engage manifested in subtle avoidance. He appeared to prefer to study and comment on objects in the psychotherapist's room rather than engaging directly with the psychotherapist. He avoided eye-contact.

The psychotherapist verbalised understanding that Matthew was likely to be thinking that he was required to attend because he was bad and because his foster parent thought so too. Matthew responded to this comment by orienting to the psychotherapist's face and smiling in acknowledgement. Having Matthew's attention, the psychotherapist then told Matthew that the intent of psychotherapy was to make him feel happier and, as such, that it would be fun.

To prove the point, the psychotherapist engaged Matthew in fun activities and games, the purpose of which were to facilitate Matthew's acceptance of it being safe and rewarding for an adult to be in control, to engage with him, to care for him and to promote his self-esteem.[26] For the remainder of the session and each session thereafter Matthew engaged enthusiastically in a psychotherapy approach that was carefully orchestrated by the psychotherapist to facilitate Matthew's acceptance of adults in a caring role, his deservedness to be cared for, his perception that adults understand and can fix most things, and his successful engagement with his broader social world.

CHAPTER SUMMARY

- Effective treatment of attachment-disordered children involves:
  - education of caregivers about the care and management requirements of the attachment-disordered child
  - education of teachers and other professionals about the care and management requirements of the attachment-disordered child; and
  - psychotherapy.

- Psychotherapy involves methodologies based on psychological theories applied to the treatment of mental disorders.

- Effective psychotherapies for attachment-disordered children include play therapies, attachment-oriented therapies and cognitive–behavioural therapies.

- Effective psychotherapy is that which focuses on strengthening the child.

- Caregiver participation in psychotherapy is important.

- Voluntary participants do better in psychotherapy.

- Attachment-disordered children are more likely to be voluntary participants in psychotherapy when:
  - they experience that adults understand their misgivings and apprehensions about attending psychotherapy
  - they are reassured that psychotherapy is being instigated in order to promote their happiness
  - they are told that psychotherapy, and the psychotherapist, is likely to be fun and validating of their interests and experience.

POSTSCRIPT

EYES ARE MIRRORS FOR A CHILD'S SOUL. WHAT DO CHILDREN SEE IN YOUR EYES?

The above parenting maxim is derived from the idea that children's self-concept is tied to how they perceive that their parents/caregivers see them. If a child experiences their parent/caregiver as having a perception of them as bad, the child will form the belief that they are bad. In contrast, if a child experiences their parent/caregiver as having a perception of them as good, the child will form a belief that they are good.

Insecure children are unsure whether they are good or bad. Attachment-disordered children perceive themselves to be bad. As long as they perceive themselves to be bad, they will act bad. Acting bad produces a predictable response in others and confirms their belief system, which is reassuring to the insecure and attachment-disordered child. It provides an element of stability and predictability to counter-balance their perception that their world is unpredictable and chaotic, this latter being anxiety-evoking. Negative conduct also draws more attention than positive conduct.

Consider the fact that newborn babies draw attention to their needs through affective displays that would later be considered as being anti-social. This behaviour, along with a gregarious smile, has emerged through evolution as an effective means by which the young child communicates with others and secures needs-provision. It follows that children who are preoccupied with accessibility to needs-provision are likely to use these infant strategies (i.e., charming smiles and screaming tantrums). We should not be surprised that these strategies are consistent with the three reported subtypes of Reactive Attachment Disorder: the inhibited–anti-social type (tantrums), the disinhibited–gregarious type (charming smiles), and the combined type (tantrums and charming smiles).

In caring for attachment-disordered children it is important to maintain a positive attitude and disposition towards the child as a person and not to be drawn into a perception of them as fundamentally bad because their behaviour is bad. Spending special time together and exclaiming over their positive qualities and abilities are useful starting points in this process, as is holding and maintaining positive thoughts about the child.

Nevertheless, it is important to be mindful that in doing so you are acting unpredictably from the child's point of view. This will take some getting used to at first for the child and they may even actively resist (e.g. 'So you think I am good; well I'll show you just how bad I can be'). Nevertheless, in the longer term they will come to accept that you see them in a positive light and this will be the beginning of them seeing themselves the same way.

GLOSSARY OF TERMS

Aberrant behaviour: Behaviour that does not conform to societal standards and, as a result, damages relationships with others.

Accessibility: Having ready, easy, reliable and consistent access to basic human needs from an adult or adults who is/are in a caregiving role.

Adaptation: Being able to live in one's social environment successfully.

Affect: Emotion.

Affective attunement: Emotional connectedness, where two people express, and otherwise appear to experience, the same or similar emotion as each other.

Affect regulation: The capacity to control intensity of emotions for one's own benefit and in order to conform to conventional standards of emotional expression.

Anxiety: A pervasive feeling of worry or uneasiness, accompanied by physiological symptoms (e.g. sweating, palpitations, restlessness), and usually associated with an exaggerated perception of threat or danger.

Arousal: In this book, 'arousal' is used to refer to rate of brain activity.

Attachment: A term used to describe the dependency relationship the child develops towards his or her primary caregivers.

Attachment figure: Someone who provides physical and emotional care, has continuity and consistency in the child's life, and who has an emotional investment in the child's life.

Attachment representations: The beliefs one has about self, others and interpersonal relationships.

Attributions: Beliefs – in this book used to denote beliefs one has about self, others and interpersonal relationships.

Attunement experience: See **Affective attunement**.

Bond: A uniting force that links people to one another.

Cognitive-behavioural therapy: A treatment methodology that is based on theories of cognition and learning and the remediation of thoughts and behaviours that precipitate and maintain maladjustment.

Compulsion: A seemingly irresistible act performed in response to an impulse. In the context of this book, the impulse in question is that of obtaining reassurance regarding accessibility to needs-provision.

Deficit attributions: Beliefs about self that relate to damage, inadequacy, impotency, and which undermine self-esteem and maintain a negative self-concept.

Dependency: When one person (in this case a child) relies on others to respond to their needs and reasonable wishes sensitively, accurately and reliably.

Detached: When a child shows an absence of emotional connectedness and dependency upon others.

Developmental deficit: Refers to a condition under which a child fails to achieve a normally expected developmental milestone.

Developmental delay: Refers to a condition whereby the development of an infant or child is slower than is normally expected.

Developmental milestone: Skills and abilities that most children learn at a certain age.

Developmental psychology: The scientific study of how children develop, including fine and gross motor development, language development, emotional development, social development, moral development, cognitive development.

Diagnosis: The process of categorising behaviour through evaluation of a person's history, presentation, the person's own reports concerning their behaviour and the reports of others who know them.

Dissociation: A process by which a person becomes detached from their immediate environment. A defence that develops in response to intolerably high levels of stress.

Empathy: A feeling of emotional connectedness to another, such that one person feels the same or similar emotion and intensity of emotion as the other.

Empirical evidence: Refers to knowledge or information that is gathered through scientific study.

Evolutionary: Used to refer to behaviour that has been selected through history as it serves a useful purpose in the survival of the species.

Hypervigilance: Being acutely aware of one's surroundings, particularly for signs of threat or danger.

Infants: Children 0–2 years of age.

Insecure attachment: An outcome whereby an infant has either failed to learn that he or she can consistently depend upon their primary caregiver(s) to love, nurture and protect them, or has learnt that he or she cannot consistently depend upon their primary caregiver(s) to love, nurture and protect them.

Interactive repair: An action on the part of a caregiving adult whereby they positively re-connect with a dependent child in association with having had to admonish the child or otherwise discipline them for engaging in inappropriate behaviour or affective displays.

Internalise: A process by which an idea becomes a semi-permanent aspect of a person's belief system.

Maladaptive: Used in connection with beliefs, behaviours and affective displays that compromise a person's success in living in their environment.

Motor development: The development of the capacity to roll, sit, crawl, walk, run, climb, jump, grasp and physically manipulate.

Naturalistic observation: Involves observing the subject in its natural environment as unobtrusively as possible.

Primary attachment relationships: The Attachment relationships the child has with his or her main caregivers.

Primary caregiver: The infant/child's main caregiver.

Primary dependency relationships: The relationship(s) between the infants and the person or persons who are their primary caregivers.

Psychoanalytic: Refers to a theory of personality, developed by Sigmund Freud, which focuses on the idea that human behaviour is governed by unconscious forces and repression of internal conflicts.

Psycho-education: A process by which people are informed about psychological theories and other psychological information relevant to a mental disorder or condition and its treatment. Psycho-education can be delivered verbally in the context of face-to-face interactions with a mental-health professional and in the form of written information (also known as 'Bibliotherapy').

Psychological: To do with the mind.

Psychology: The science of the mind or mental life.

Psychotherapy: The use of psychological theories and methods in the treatment of mental disorders.

Secure attachment: An outcome whereby an infant has learnt that he or she can consistently depend upon their primary caregiver(s) to love, nurture and protect them.

Socialisation: The process of learning about the culture of one's social world and how to live in accordance with it.

Startle response: A physical, emotional and cognitive response to an unexpected event, such as a flash of light or a loud noise, whereby the infant reacts with sudden movements of the arms and legs, blinking and in some instances, emotional distress.

Stranger reaction: Usually observed in infants and young children, it is recognised in the child seeking closeness or otherwise orienting to their primary attachment figures in the presence of a person who is relatively unknown to them. The classic sign of the stranger reaction is when young children stand slightly behind and cling to their parent's leg while shyly gazing at a relatively unknown person.

Therapeutic alliance: The creation of a particular relationship between the mental-health professional and the patient that is specifically boundaried in order to ensure that the work of psychotherapy can be carried out effectively.

Time-out: A form of punishment whereby a child is temporarily sent to a place where they are excluded from interaction with others, usually for the same number of minutes as their chronological age.

Trauma: An emotional or psychological injury, usually resulting from an extremely stressful or upsetting life-experience.

ABOUT THE AUTHOR

Colby Pearce is the Principal Psychologist at Secure Start, a private psychology practice specialising in the provision of psychological services to children, adolescents and families. A graduate of the University of Adelaide, he was first registered to practise as a psychologist in 1995. His work since registration has incorporated the provision of assessment and psychotherapy services in the areas of child protection, family law, inter-country adoption, refugees and community child and family psychology. He was the founder and Director of the Child Well-being Clinics, Master of Psychology training clinics that operated between 2006 and 2008 as a joint initiative between the University of South Australia and Families SA, and which provided a psychology service to abused, neglected and traumatised children.

Colby has extensive experience in teaching and training of psychologists and other professionals and seven international publications about adolescent mental health. His 1994 publication *Predicting Suicide Attempts Among Adolescents* contributed to an Australia-wide general practitioner education and awareness programme concerning adolescent suicidality. He is regularly called upon to speak about the care and management of traumatised and attachment-disordered children. He is married with three young children.

ENDNOTES

1. Howes, C., Hamilton, C.E. and Althusen, V. (unpublished). 'Using the Attachment Q-Set to Describe Non-familial Attachments.' Cited by C. Howes (1999) 'Attachment Relationships in the Context of Multiple Caregivers.' In J. Cassidy and P.R. Shaver (eds) *Handbook of Attachment: Theory, Research and Clinical Applications.* New York, NY: The Guilford Press.

2. Howes, C. (1999) 'Attachment Relationships in the Context of Multiple Caregivers.' In J. Cassidy and P.R. Shaver (eds) *Handbook of Attachment: Theory, Research and Clinical Applications.* New York, NY: The Guilford Press.

3. Harlow, H.F. (1958) The nature of love.' *American Psychologist 13,* 673–685.

4. Ainsworth, M., Blehar, M., Waters, E. and Wall, S. (1978) *Patterns of Attachment: A Psychological Study of the Strange Situation.* Hillsdale, NJ: Laurence Erlbaum and Associates.

5. Bowlby, J. (1969) *Attachment and Loss. Volume I: Attachment.* New York: Basic Books.

6. Bowlby, J. (1973) *Attachment and Loss. Volume II: Separation.* New York: Basic Books.

7. Ainsworth, M., Blehar, M., Waters, E. and Wall, S. (1978) *Patterns of Attachment: A Psychological Study of the Strange Situation.* Hillsdale, NJ: Laurence Erlbaum and Associates.

8. Delaney, R.J. (1994) *Fostering Changes: Treating Attachment-Disordered Foster Children.* Fort Collins, CO: Corbett.

9. Bowlby, J. (1982) 'Attachment and loss: retrospect and prospect.' *American Journal of Orthopsychiatry 52,* 4, 664–678.

10. Delaney, R.J. (1994) *Fostering Changes: Treating Attachment-Disordered Foster Children.* Fort Collins, CO: Corbett.

11. Ainsworth, M., Blehar, M., Waters, E. and Wall, S. (1978) *Patterns of Attachment: A Psychological Study of the Strange Situation.* Hillsdale, NJ: Laurence Erlbaum and Associates.

12. Ainsworth, M., Blehar, M., Waters, E. and Wall, S. (1978) *Patterns of Attachment: A Psychological Study of the Strange Situation.* Hillsdale, NJ: Laurence Erlbaum and Associates.

13. Ainsworth, M., Blehar, M., Waters, E. and Wall, S. (1978) *Patterns of Attachment: A Psychological Study of the Strange Situation.* Hillsdale, NJ: Laurence Erlbaum and Associates.

14. Ainsworth, M., Blehar, M., Waters, E. and Wall, S. (1978) *Patterns of Attachment: A Psychological Study of the Strange Situation.* Hillsdale, NJ: Laurence Erlbaum and Associates.

15. Main, M. and Solomon, J. (1990) 'Procedures for Identifying Infants as Disorganised/Disoriented during Ainsworth Strange Situations.' In M.T. Greenberg, D. Cicchetti, and E.M. Cummings (eds) *Attachment in the Preschool Years: Theory, Research and Intervention.* Chicago, IL: University of Chicago Press.

16. Delaney, R.J. (1994) *Fostering Changes: Treating Attachment-Disordered Foster Children.* Fort Collins, CO: Corbett.

17. Delaney, R.J. (1994) *Fostering Changes: Treating Attachment-Disordered Foster Children.* Fort Collins, CO: Corbett.

18. Reite, M. and Field, T. (eds) (1985) *The Psychobiology of Attachment And Separation.* Orlando, FL: Academic Press.

19. At five months of age a child is beginning to discriminate between familiar and unfamiliar adults, but has yet to form an attachment to anyone.

20. Howes, C., Hamilton, C.E. and Althusen, V. (unpublished). 'Using the Attachment Q-Set to Describe Non-familial Attachments.' Cited by C. Howes (1999) 'Attachment Relationships in the Context of Multiple Caregivers.' In J. Cassidy and P.R. Shaver (eds) *Handbook of Attachment: Theory, Research and Clinical Applications.* New York, NY: The Guilford Press.

21. Delaney, R.J. (1994) *Fostering Changes: Treating Attachment-Disordered Foster Children.* Fort Collins, CO: Corbett.

22. Bretherton, I., Ridgeway, D. and Cassidy, J. (1990) 'Assessing internal working models of the attachment relationship: An attachment story completion task for 3-year-olds.' In M. Greenberg, D. Cicchetti and E. Cummings (eds) *Attachment in the Preschool Years: Theory, Research and Intervention* (pp.273–310). Chicago, IL: University of Chicago Press.

23. Speltz, M. (1990) 'The treatment of preschool conduct problems: An integration of behavioural and attachment concepts.' In M. Greenberg, D. Cicchetti and E. Cummings (eds) *Attachment in the Preschool Years: Theory, Research and Intervention* (pp.399–426). Chicago, IL: University of Chicago Press.

24. Delaney, R.J. (1994) *Fostering Changes: Treating Attachment-Disordered Foster Children.* Fort Collins, CO: Corbett.

25. See Jernberg, A.M., and Booth, P.B. (2001) *Theraplay: Helping Parents and Children Build Better Relationships Through Attachment-Based Play* (2nd edn). San Francisco, CA: Jossey Bass.

26. Jernberg, A.M. and Booth, P.B. (2001) *Theraplay: Helping Parents and Children Build Better Relationships Through Attachment-Based Play* (2nd edn). San Francisco, CA: Jossey Bass.

INDEX